KT-529-674

GOING
PUBLIC

GOING PUBLIC

edited by
JONATHAN REUVID

RECOMMENDED BY
INSTITUTE OF DIRECTORS

www.pinsents.com

Grant Thornton

BINNS AND COMPANY

CORPORATE AND FINANCIAL PUBLIC RELATIONS

KOGAN
PAGE

This book has been endorsed by the Institute of Directors. The endorsement is given to selected Kogan Page books which the IoD recognizes as being of specific interest to its members and providing them with up-to-date, informative and practical resources for creating business success. Kogan Page books endorsed by the IoD represent the most authoritative guidance available on a wide range of subjects including management, finance, marketing, training and HR.

The views expressed in this book are those of the authors and are not necessarily the same as those of the Institute of Directors.

First published in 2003

Apart from any fair dealing for the purposes of research or private study, or criticism or review, as permitted under the Copyright, Designs and Patents Act 1988, this publication may only be reproduced, stored or transmitted, in any form or by any means, with the prior permission in writing of the publishers, or in the case of reprographic reproduction in accordance with the terms and licences issued by the CLA. Enquiries concerning reproduction outside these terms should be sent to the publishers at the undermentioned address:

Kogan Page Limited
120 Pentonville Road
London N1 9JN
United Kingdom

www.kogan-page.co.uk

© Kogan Page, 2003

British Library Cataloguing in Publication Data

A CIP record for this book is available from the British Library.

ISBN 0 7494 3920 3

Typeset by Saxon Graphics Ltd, Derby
Printed and bound in Great Britain by Clays Ltd, St Ives plc

33 FTSE 100 clients

18 Fortune 500 clients

19 AIM clients

Top 10 ranked legal adviser to UK public listed companies

Top 20 adviser on M & A deals in 2001

Top 5 ranked firm by in-house counsel

550+ lawyers

160+ partners

Pin
numbers

Few law firms have our depth and breadth of experience in advising UK Plcs, or in bringing companies to market.

If you're planning a listing on the main market or AIM, call Martin Shaw, Andrew Eastgate or Gareth Edwards on 0845 300 32 32.

MOST ENTERPRISING LAW FIRM · LEGAL BUSINESS · AWARD WINNER 2002

Pinsent Curtis Biddle

www.pinsents.com

Is your business at a crossroads? Not sure which way to turn for the financial advice that will shape your future? Then **Grant Thornton Corporate Finance...**

Grant Thornton

...will lead you along the best route. Let us help you put together the bespoke financial package that will help your business grow in the right direction.

For more information contact:
Philip Secrett
Grant Thornton Corporate Finance
Grant Thornton House
Melton Street
London NW1 2EP
T 0870 991 2578
E philip.j.secrett@gtuk.com

Grant Thornton, the UK member of
Grant Thornton International, is authorised by
the Financial Services Authority.
© 2002 Grant Thornton. All rights reserved.
www.grant-thornton.co.uk

Contents

Notes on contributors

PINSENT CURTIS BIDDLE

Pinsent Curtis Biddle is a top ten legal adviser to UK public listed companies and has been ranked in the top five nationally for client service by UK in-house lawyers. In the Legal Business 2002 Awards it received the accolade of the UK's 'Most Enterprising Law Firm'.

The firm acts for 35 FTSE 100 companies, more than 70 companies in the FTSE 350 and extensively for foreign controlled companies, including 18 Fortune 500 corporations. More than 60 of their partners are independently rated for their expertise.

Pinsent Curtis Biddle has more than 160 partners, a full legal team of more than 550 and a total UK staff of over 1,000 based in London, Birmingham, Leeds and Manchester. Internationally, it has alliances in France, Germany and Sweden, reinforced by extensive links in the US and the rest of Europe.

Martin Shaw is a partner in Pinsent Curtis Biddle and is Head of Corporate in Leeds with a wealth of corporate finance experience. He has advised extensively on stock exchange related matters, including full listings, AiM and OFEX admissions, takeovers governed by the City Code and fund-raising including secondary issues as well as a broad range of mergers, acquisitions and company reorganizations. He acts for a number of major UK clients and has wide experience of transactions in Europe and the United States.

Andrew Black is an Associate in the Corporate Department in Leeds, specializing in public company work. He also advises on flotations, placings, rights issues and takeovers as well as acquisitions and disposals for both public and private companies.

Hannah Kendrick is an Associate in Leeds specializing principally in corporate finance work advising companies and their institutional advisers on fund-raising; flotations and further issues including placings, open offers and rights issues as well as advising both listed and unlisted companies on acquisitions and disposals. She is also is a member of the firm's specialist Life Sciences Team.

Philip Goldsborough is an Associate in the Corporate department in Leeds and is a member of the Corporate Finance team. He has experience in a wide range of corporate finance transactions, including flotations, placings and open offers, takeovers, rights issues, demergers and numerous acquisitions and disposals for both listed and unlisted companies.

Andrew Walker is a senior corporate partner in Leeds and a former head of Corporate. He specializes in all aspects of company law particularly corporate finance, Stock Exchange issues, corporate reorganizations and M&As in the UK and internationally. He is a nationally rated expert advising a number of listed and private companies as well as acting on MBOs and MBIs.

GRANT THORNTON

Grant Thornton is one of the world's leading organizations of accounting and consulting firms providing assurance, tax and specialist advice to owner-managed businesses and their owners and to fast-growing, entrepreneurial people and businesses.

The strength of each local firm is reflected in the quality of the organization. Grant Thornton operates in over 100 countries, bringing together 20,000 personnel in 600 offices worldwide where experienced professionals combine local market knowledge with technically advanced systems. All firms share a commitment to providing the same high quality service to their clients wherever they choose to do business.

Nick Jeffrey qualified as a Chartered Accountant with a mid-tier firm in 1996, before joining Grant Thornton. He is a manager on secondment to the Client Services Support Department, where he specializes in issues facing Smaller Quoted Companies.

Colin Aaronson spent twelve years in industry after qualifying as a Chartered Accountant, most recently as the Finance Director of a telecoms group with operations in Europe and Asia. He joined the Capital Markets team as a manager in January 2000 and has completed a number of AiM flotations and takeovers. Colin specializes in advising technology businesses.

Ruth Cooke is a senior technical manager with the Client Services Support Department. She worked in the Institute of Chartered Accountants of England & Wales (ICAEW) for ten years in a variety of technical roles before joining Grant Thornton. Prior to the ICAEW, she worked for firms of all sizes in different audit and technical areas in various parts of the world.

Richard Harwood is a Senior Pensions Manager based in Grant Thornton's West Yorkshire Office. He is Chairman of the firm's Designated Pensions Specialist and runs the West Yorkshire Pensions Unit.

Richard joined Grant Thornton in 1999 and brought with him many years of experience in a wide range of pensions-related matters, having previously worked in a pensions capacity at insurance companies and employee benefits consultants.

Robert Langston is a Chartered Tax Adviser who joined Grant Thornton's Kettering office in 1998 to give tax advice to mid-corporate businesses and their owners. He currently works in the firm's Client Services Support Department, providing technical support to client-facing partners and staff.

Naomi Sharma is a Senior Manager based in Grant Thornton's London Corporate Finance department. She specializes in due diligence, focusing on flotation and public company transactions.

BINNS & CO

Binns & Co is a full service, financial and corporate public relations and investor relations consultancy based in the City of London with international affiliates in all of the world's key financial centres. It is a member of The Worldcom Group, the world's largest network of independently-owned Public Relations agencies. Binns & Co. draws on imagination, experience and professionalism to create effective communications programmes that add value to clients' businesses. It ranks among Britain's top ten financial public relations consultancies.

Peter Binns is Executive Chairman of Binns & Co. After seven years in US newspaper and UK business and financial journalism, he moved into private client stockbroking and then into international and City public relations from 1979. Having started in London, at Burson-Marsteller, Peter Binns established Binns & Co in 1994 via a management buy-out.

ROBERT W BAIRD

Robert W Baird Limited ('Baird') is an international investment banking, private equity, asset and wealth management firm. Established in 1919, Baird has over 2,500 associates located in 80 offices throughout the United States and Europe.

In the United Kingdom Baird focuses on the small and mid-cap market, providing advice to a wide range of companies and institutions using its equity research, institutional sales and investment banking expertise.

Shaun Dobson, Director Investment Banking, Head of Technology, joined Baird in July 2000. He ran the Applied Technology team before being given the additional responsibility of heading the enlarged Technology team in November 2001. For the preceding 12 years Shaun worked for Credit Lyonnais Securities (formerly Laing & Cruickshank), being appointed director in 1997. Assignments during his career have include the flotation of and subsequent fund-raisings/acquisitions for Capita, acting as corporate broker on the recommended offer for the GRE, to the Royal Bank of Scotland on its successful hostile bid for National Westminster Bank, acting on new issues including Games Workshop, GAME, AMS and a large number of secondary issues including Persimmon and API. Whilst at Baird, in addition to advising on specific transactions, Shaun has been involved in increasing the company's list of corporate clients.

ABOUT THE EDITOR

Jonathan Reuvid is consultant editor and part-author of a series of international business books and of titles relating to the finance and business management of UK small and medium sized enterprises, all published by Kogan Page.

Foreword

Flotation is one of the biggest milestones in a company's development. It is a major event, inevitably bringing about substantial and permanent change to the nature of the organization.

It can be hugely satisfying – and rewarding – for all those involved, but it is a big and (usually) irreversible step, often with consequences that were neither sought nor foreseen.

Flotation needs to be approached carefully. The underlying goals have to be clear; the alternative routes to their achievement need to be evaluated; the emotion and the ego need to be set aside; the timing needs to be thoughtfully judged; the advisers have to be carefully chosen; and the whole process has to be properly managed. Indeed the manner of execution is as vital to success as the appropriateness of the original decision.

From personal experience of two flotations, I can say that there are few more satisfying achievements in running a business, but you need to go into it with your eyes open.

This book sets out to give practical guidance to all considering this challenging route forward.

George Cox
Director General, Institute of Directors

Introduction

The directors and shareholders of most successful and growing companies examine the opportunities to 'go public' at least once in their business lifetime. What may have been originally little more than a budding entrepreneur's aspiration becomes a realistic alternative as the company evolves and generates a track record. In the UK, with its sophisticated hierarchy of stock markets under the jurisdiction of the London Stock Exchange, dynamic start-up businesses may apply for early admission to the lower tier markets of OFEX or AiM. Even admission to the Full List requires a minimum financial track record of no more than three years.

An introduction to the flotation alternative is given in the public equity section of *The Corporate Finance Handbook* (Kogan Page, 2001) but the directors and owners of a business will need much more detail to examine thoroughly whether flotation offers the most appropriate financial strategy at the current stage of their company's development and is likely to provide optimum long-term benefits for shareholders.

Going Public: The essential guide to flotation issues, the latest in the Kogan Page series of business titles endorsed by the Institute of

1

Directors, is divided into three distinct parts. The first focuses on the basic decision-making discussion of whether or not to float. Alternative financial strategies and sources of finance are examined, as well as the necessary and sufficient conditions for flotation against the present equity investment environment. All directors and shareholders engaging in the strategic debate will find the detailed information they need to participate intelligently. If the outcome of the debate is to delay flotation, then the ingredients for revisiting the issue will remain the same and are all contained in this book.

The second part examines the flotation process in detail, including the roles of each of the key professional advisers and practitioners that a company will need to engage for an application to list and a successful flotation. The complex techniques of company share valuation and taxation issues will be of most interest to financial directors, but all directors of the company are involved in the flotation process in varying degrees and share collectively in responsibility for the accuracy of the prospectus, accounting and other documents. The amount of time and degree of involvement required in the process, in a period when directors will be striving to deliver company best performance, may seem daunting.

The third part of the book dwells on life with the listing. The company's status as a public listed company brings with it new obligations in terms of financial reporting, auditing, corporate governance and communication as well as the benefits and perils of a higher public profile. There will be additional administrative costs and demands on directors' time and increased pressures to deliver ever-improving financial performance.

The final chapter of the book discusses the realization of shareholder value from the listing and the tax implications of holding and disposal of listed shares. These topics address the ultimate aims of owner-directors in achieving personal wealth, which can only be gained through completing flotation successfully and maintaining responsible stewardship of the company thereafter.

Each chapter of the book has been written by an experienced professional practitioner from a leading firm in the relevant field.

We are especially grateful to Martin Shaw of Pinsent Curtis Biddle, the original architect of the book, and to him and his colleagues for authoring chapters in Parts II and III relating to regulatory and legal matters and the obligations of directors. I am indebted to Colin Aaronson of Grant Thornton for the whole of Part I and to him and his colleagues for key contributions to Parts II and III. Shaun Dobson of Robert W Baird Limited provided the chapter on the broker's role and Peter Binns of Binns & Co has written a practical guide to the role of corporate public relations in flotations as the closing contribution to Part II.

Going Public: The essential guide to flotation issues is sponsored by Pinsent Curtis Biddle, Grant Thornton and Binns & Co, whose support Kogan Page acknowledges gratefully. Finally, we thank George Cox, Director General of the Institute of Directors for his Foreword. We hope that company directors, shareholders and those who advise them will find the book a useful addition to their business bookshelves.

Jonathan Reuvid
September 2002

Part I

To float or not to float – planning your company's future

1

The equity environment

Colin Aaronson (Grant Thornton)

SUMMARY

- Benign conditions led to an 18-year bull market from 1982 to 2000, as inflation fell from 8.5 to 2.1 per cent.[1] *i.e. Capital growth*
- Those conditions were also extremely favourable for raising money through flotations, particularly from 1998 to 2000.
- The outlook going forward is uncertain. Unless conditions remain benign as they did overall throughout the 1980s and 1990s, we cannot expect to see the same level of capital growth as took place in that period. Where capital growth is less certain, investors will place an increased emphasis on yield.
- Opportunities exist to float and raise money for good businesses, but investors are likely to look for a strong earnings stream, ideally underpinned by long-term contracts, at a price that represents good value.
- Raising money for ideas is considerably more difficult than in the years leading up to the millennium, when the dot com boom

was at its peak. There is still money for pre-profit and even pre-revenue businesses, but the business and the people behind it must be of particularly high quality.

INTRODUCTION

When is it a good time to raise money through a flotation?

Companies do raise money in both bull and bear markets, although investor interest will be greater when confidence is high and share prices are increasing. The period from 1982 to 2000, and the 1990s in particular, were especially favourable for raising money in the City and in other financial markets. It was not an entirely smooth ride for investors, with the overall trend line punctuated by blips in individual market sectors and the market as a whole. At the height of the boom in 1999 and 2000, brokers were so busy raising money that the problem was not finding the money but getting an appointment. Those same brokers are now available for lunch, and some even for interview.

As merger and acquisition (M&A) and Initial Public Offering (IPO) activity abated, investment banks and brokers and other professional firms laid off or redeployed staff. Activity is at a lower level in 2002 than in 2000 but deals are still taking place, and from early in 2002 a number of large private companies signalled that they intended to come to the market. Even in recession flotations did not stop happening.

The outlook in 2002 is uncertain and the long term effect of corporate failures such as Enron and Marconi, unclear. Inflation and interest rates cannot go down much further, and political events worldwide are capable of dealing a blow to even the most robust recovery.

Investors have never really had it so good as they did in the years 1988 to 2000. An investor who put money into an index fund at the start of 1988 would have seen £1,000 reach over £4,000 by the millennium,[2] whilst average house buyers would have seen the value of their home increase by 69 per cent. Companies found it easier to raise equity capital than ever before. In 1988, £3,790 million

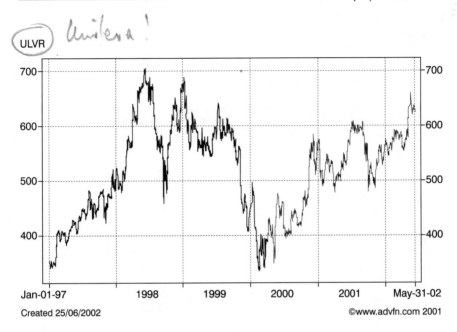

Figure 1.1 *FTSE-100 1997–2002*

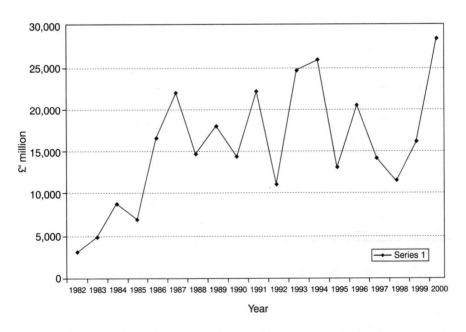

Figure 1.2 *Funds raised in London (excluding Eurobonds)*

Table 1.1 *Funds raised in London*

	Total listed		New Companies		Other Issues		Eurobonds		AIM		USM		Excluding Eurobonds
	No.	Money Raised (£m)	No. of Co.'s	Money Raised (£m)	No. of Issues	Money Raised (£m)	No. of Issues	Money Raised (£m)	No. of Issues	Money Raised (£m)	No. of Issues	Money Raised (£m)	
UK & Irish													
1980	2,359	1,647.0	35	240.7	2,324	1,379.3	n/a	27.0			n/a	14.0	
1981	2,267	2,909.0	63	631.3	2,204	2,277.7	—	—			n/a	86.8	
1982	1,890	3,018.9	59	1,168.5	1,831	1,750.4	n/a	100.0			n/a	118.6	3,038
1983	2,519	4,580.2	79	1,591.6	2,440	2,918.6	n/a	70.0			n/a	252.4	4,763
1984	3,094	9,001.3	87	5,950.2	3,007	2,531.1	n/a	520.0			n/a	261.7	8,743
1985	3,242	13,845.8	80	1,462.2	2,941	5,144.7	221	7,238.9			n/a	344.6	6,952
1986	4,111	23,249.0	136	8,874.2	3,760	7,267.8	215	7,107.0			n/a	446.1	16,588
1987	4,883	26,655.7	155	5,002.4	4,633	16,042.8	95	5,610.5			n/a	935.3	21,981
1988	4,072	19,858.4	129	3,789.9	3,872	9,944.5	71	6,124.0			575	1,019.0	14,753
1989	3,956	26,580.7	110	7,578.1	3,749	9,557.0	97	9,445.6			661	851.9	17,987
1990	3,205	27,853.7	120	7,094.9	2,953	6,783.9	132	13,974.9			453	507.1	14,386
1991	3,319	35,131.1	101	7,474.1	2,985	14,287.1	233	13,369.9			319	377.5	22,139
1992	2,876	24,234.2	82	2,937.0	2,488	7,940.6	306	13,356.6			277	202.7	11,080
1993	2,655	49,134.8	180	5,966.3	1,941	18,422.8	534	24,745.7			212	309.4	24,699
1994	3,168	57,523.7	256	11,519.3	1,978	13,943.0	934	32,061.4			202	461.8	25,924

Table 1.1 *contd*

	Total listed		New Companies		Other Issues		Eurobonds		AIM		USM		
	No.	Money Raised (£m)	No. of Co.'s	Money Raised (£m)	No. of Issues	Money Raised (£m)	No. of Issues	Money Raised (£m)	No. of Issues	Money Raised (£m)	No. of Issues	Money Raised (£m)	Money Raised Excluding Eurobonds
UK only													
1995	2,803	37,573.0	190	2,961.7	1,710	9,845.6	903	24,765.7	162	94.8	99	211.6	13,114
1996	3,029	55,192.5	230	10,607.2	1,773	8,924.2	1,026	35,661.1	388	816.1	55	179.6	20,527
1997	2,788	57,213.3	135	7,100.3	1,486	6,468.7	1,167	43,644.4	454	694.5			14,263
1998	1,901	66,751.1	124	4,196.2	851	6,779.7	926	55,775.2	432	557.6			11,533
1999	2,023	100,785.5	106	5,353.4	895	9,916.7	1,022	85,515.3	562	933.4			16,204
2000	2,081	125,934.1	172	11,399.2	897	13,978.8	1,012	100,556.1	1,038	3,073.8			28,452
2001	1,917	105,088.0	113	6,921.7	869	14,824.2	935	83,342.1	787	1,128.1			

** *For years 1981 to 1992 non-money raising issues are included. From 1993 only money raising issues are shown.*

Source: London Stock Exchange

was raised through flotation in London; by 2000, that figure had become £11,399 million.[3] Yet things would have looked very different in October 1987.

THE EXUBERANT 1980s

The 1980s saw a vigorous recovery following the severe recession of 1980–82. The liberalization of financial markets had led to a rapid growth in consumer spending fuelled by growing confidence and funded by easy credit. Share prices rose on the back of improved company performance and the confidence that came from the sense that things really were different under Conservative governments on both sides of the Atlantic. It really did feel like morning in the United States and the UK, open for business. Share prices in both London and on Wall Street rose by approximately 250 per cent between January 1982 and September 1987.

In the 'can do' economy that Britain was becoming, wealth creation became fashionable again and, spurred by privatization windfalls, equity investment became an activity practised by ever-larger numbers of people. Greed apparently became a virtue and even the leader of the Labour Party wondered if 'yuppies' might be a suitable role model. Investment banking became more global and overseas financial institutions moved into London to take advantage of the new opportunities. This inflow of institutions and people enlarged the skill base and deepened the pool of capital available in London. The old order finally gave way to the new in 1986 as 'Big Bang' did away with independent jobbers, brokers and merchant banks and combined them (or at least most of them) into large multi-function investment houses. These houses played an important role in the events that were to follow, thanks in large part to their computerized dealing systems.

Five years of growth in equity prices came to an abrupt end on 19 October 1987 as share prices suffered the sharpest one-day fall since 1929. By the time prices had stabilized on 9 November, the FTSE-100 had fallen by 36 per cent from its high on 16 July 1987. There were widespread fears that the reverse 'wealth effect' of falling stock prices would cause such a contraction in consumer spending that the crash of 1987 would be followed by a depression that mirrored the great depression of the 1930s. Like his counterpart in Washington, the Chancellor of the Exchequer lowered interest rates in an attempt to support demand. House prices continued rising for a while, but by 1988 they had also begun to fall, and the phrase 'negative equity' entered our vocabulary.

We now know that the crash of 1987 did not reflect a fundamental re-appraisal of our economic prospects but was a stock market 'correction', amplified and accelerated by programme trading. Share prices had indeed reached a level at which a correction was in order, but the scale of the adjustment was both unprecedented and unforeseen in terms of its speed and magnitude; an adjustment that would previously have taken two years, took place in the space of less than four weeks. As investors clambered out from among the wreckage of the previous week's hurricanes to survey their battered investments, they would have been justified in fearing the worst; things simply would never be the same. As it happened, they got even better – so much so that 1987 represented one of the greatest investment opportunities in history.

With hindsight, we can see that between 1987 and 2000 there existed a set of conditions that would support the relentless increase in share prices. During these years when the FTSE-100 index rose by almost 300 per cent,[4] GDP increased by 36 per cent,[5] corporate profitability improved and the average P/E ratio doubled. Dividend yields fell from 3.73 per cent to 2.80 per cent.[6]

THE BENIGN ENVIRONMENT

Crucial to the steady increase in share prices was the fall in inflation. The sharp recession in 1980–82, exacerbated by tight monetary policy, had dampened demand for goods and labour and put pressure on the price of both. When the recovery did take place, there was a new approach to industrial relations as a result of the recession and the Thatcher government's confrontation with the unions, which meant that wage demands were more moderate than they had been in the 1970s.

The period was also marked by a reduction in raw material prices, notably crude oil prices, which fell from approximately \$45 per barrel in 1982 to circa $20 per barrel in 1987. By 1998, the price of oil had fallen to approximately $13 per barrel.[7] Falling commodity prices increased corporate profitability and reduced inflation. As inflation fell, interest rates followed suit and share prices rose to let dividend yields follow interest rates.

Advances in information technology were dramatic and had profound consequences for the service sector and the people who worked in it. The increased power and availability of information technology did lead to the elimination of certain types of clerical work, but they also made possible the dramatic growth of financial services and led to the creation of whole new industries, based around personal computers and call centres. These industries created more jobs than were lost. Employment in manufacturing industry was still in long-term decline, but demand for services was rising, creating jobs in tourism, design, childcare, catering and

Changes in Bank Rates, Minimum Lending Rate, Mininum Brand 1 Dealing Rate and Repo Rate

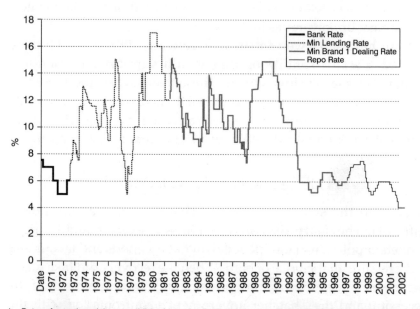

1 - Data refer to the minimum published rate the Bank discounted bills to relieve money market shortages (excludes late assistance and repurchase and sale agreements).
2 - 16.9.92, UK leaves the European Exchange Rate Mechanism. MLR set at 12%, raised to 15% (with effect from 17.9.92; never implemented).

Source: Bank of England

Figure 1.3 *Interest rates*

domestic service. Computer technology could be applied to consumer goods, which became more exciting and desirable, generating profits for companies that could design, create and distribute these products, and jobs for those who worked in them. Spending on leisure increased by 64 per cent between 1982 and 1987, and by 184 per cent between 1987 and 2000.[8]

Share prices and property prices were not only driven by positive fundamentals: they were buoyed by the need for money to find a home. Pension funds enjoyed huge tax advantages and grew in size from £84 billion in 1982 to £228 billion in 1987. By 2000 the equivalent value was £699 billion.[9] The only investments that could realistically provide the levels of growth that these funds sought were equities and property. Other money was also looking for a place to go. Fortunes made in the Klondike that was Russia after the collapse of communism found their way to Europe and the United States, accompanied by wealth that was leaving Hong Kong prior to its return to China in 1997.

The privatization of British Telecom and other nationally owned utilities and businesses in the 1980s had introduced the British public to share ownership. The introduction of Personal Equity Plans (PEPs) gave even greater incentive to individuals to invest in shares. We were becoming a share-owning democracy. Some of this money found its way into the Stock Market where it supported share prices and, aided and abetted by City executives anxious to generate fees, funded new issues.

THE END OF THE BULL MARKET

The bull market had begun to run out of steam in 1998 as the market reacted to the shocks of the Long Term Capital Management collapse and the Russian economic crisis, which had been foreshadowed by the Far Eastern economic crisis and stock market crash of 1987. Prices of a number of 'old economy' stocks had fallen in the two years to March 2000, but the market as a whole was to increase dramatically thanks to a phenomenon that became known variously as the 'dot com boom' and the 'TMT bubble' (technology, media and telecomms). Underlying this phenomenon was the increase in value of major technology and telecomms companies such as Vodafone.

The high profile factor was the dot com phenomenon. The Internet represented for many the great new 'virtual' frontier and, as Internet access became cheaper and more widespread, people left highly paid jobs in the City and elsewhere to go prospecting in the ether. Driven by greed and the fear of missing out on an opportunity that no one really understood, millions were poured into businesses that had no history, no immediate or even foreseeable prospect of making a profit, and in some cases run by people with no relevant experience. Some people believed that the world had changed and that it was now appropriate to talk of a new paradigm. Some of the companies coming to market in this brave new world had no revenue and no clear idea where that revenue was going to come from. As new measures were developed for valuing these businesses, marketing companies became 'technology' stocks, aerospace companies became 'old economy', and a loss-making

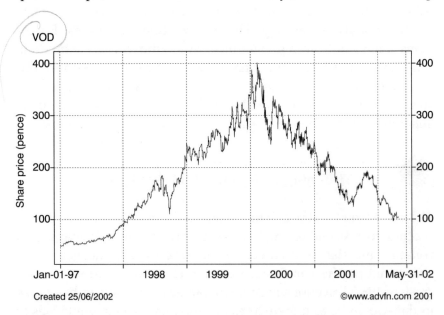

Figure 1.4a *Vodaphone*

ULVR — *Unilever*

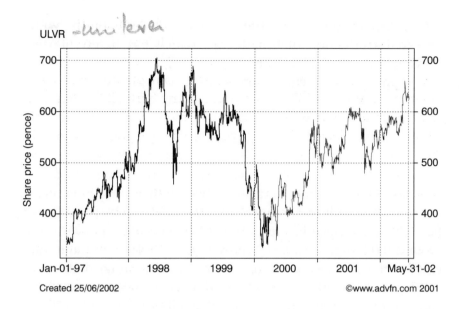

Jan-01-97   1998   1999   2000   2001   May-31-02

Created 25/06/2002   ©www.advfn.com 2001

Figure 1.4b *Unilever*

margin (?)

(virtual) bookshop became more valuable than the world's largest aircraft manufacturer. Private investors were among the keenest to subscribe to new issues, and brokers were reporting an almost insatiable investor appetite for new issues. It was intoxicating and hugely enjoyable while it lasted, but it could not go on forever. Eventually people began to realize and then acknowledge that the emperor was indeed wearing no clothes; when that happened investors lost confidence and share price graphs took on a precipice-like appearance, as stocks went into free fall, losing 90 per cent or more of their value.

To a small extent the collapse of technology stocks was the elimination of froth, but behind the collapse lay something more fundamental. The large telecommunications companies had assumed near crippling levels of debt as they attempted to outbid each other in acquiring 3G licenses, and in many cases had no cash left to fund the roll-out of new networks. Barriers to entry have been lowered, and telecomms operators face intense competition both from other operators and from the Internet. Much of the Internet's potential to

17

deliver entertainment and other services depends on the wide-spread introduction of broadband, which has barely started. Inevitably, the price of telecomms stocks fell, as did the share prices of equipment manufacturers and software companies.

AiM

The start-up dot coms were exactly the sort of business that AiM was designed for: young, smaller and riskier than companies on the Full List, but with the potential for spectacular growth. AiM had been a success since its creation in 1995, admitting an average of around 100 companies a year. The height of the dot com boom coincided with its busiest period of activity. Activity has fallen dramatically since 2000, but on an annualized basis, admissions in 2002 are running at a level similar to that of the late 1990s.

To some extent this represents a return to a more normal state of affairs. It also shows the continuing enthusiasm for the market, which admitted more companies in 2001 than the Full List, Nasdaq and Neuermarkt combined.

Table 1.2 *Number of companies on AiM*

AIM		Equities		Fixed Interest	
Date	No. of Companies	No. of Secs.	Market Value (£m)	No. of Secs.	Nominal Value (£m)
31.12.95	121	129	2,382.4	14	66.2
31.12.96	252	253	5,298.5	24	82.0
31.12.97	308	309	5,655.1	25	92.9
31.12.98	312	311	4,437.9	20	94.0
31.12.99	347	364	13,468.5	22	102.2
31.12.00	524	535	14,935.2	15	69.1
31.12.01	629	602	11,607.2	15	36.2

Source: London Stock Exchange

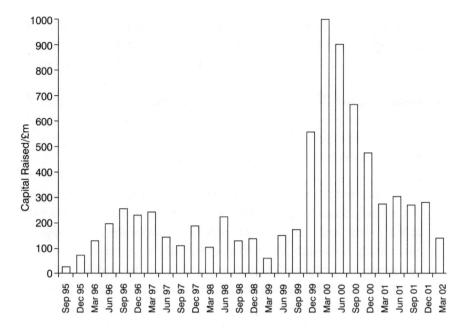

Figure 1.5 *Funds raised on AiM*

LOOKING FORWARD

So where are we now?

- Interest rates are at a 38-year low. At 30 June 2002 they were 4 per cent – and at that level there is only limited scope for improvement. If the UK does join the Euro, it will benefit from European-style interest rates. (It is widely agreed that Sterling will need to devalue before the UK can join the Euro, and interest rates would have to fall for that to happen.)
- But there are forces that may lead to increased interest rates. There appears to be a consensus that the combination of a growing population and restrictions on house building caused by planning regulations will continue to drive UK house prices upwards. This may well increase investor interest in property at the expense of equities, but some sectors such as construction, house building and property may thrive. Wage inflation is running ahead of the increase in the RPI and, combined with

house price inflation, may force the Bank of England to raise interest rates. Interest rates may also increase if the government is unable to fund increases in public expenditure through taxation.

- If capital growth in the market does not recur to the same extent as it did between 1987 and 2000, investors are going to place greater emphasis on dividend yields. This is likely to increase investor interest in bonds at the expense of equities.

- Shares being offered at IPO are priced to attract potential investors, with the result that they generally go to a premium. As a result those lucky enough to get shares in an IPO expect to make an instant profit, either paper or cash (if they are 'stags'). Shares in IPOs are therefore generally offered to brokers' favoured institutional, and occasionally, private clients.

  A feature of the dot com boom was the large number of private individuals buying shares in dot coms and other high risk companies at IPO; many have lost considerable amounts of money in the process. Consequently, there is a reluctance on the part of private investors to invest any money at all in IPOs at the present time. So, it is back to the professionals who are still prepared to invest in companies provided that the investment proposition is sound. Although there are exceptions – such as mineral exploration or biotechnology – the businesses in which investors will invest are generally the same types of business that they have traditionally looked for: well managed, *already* profitable companies with significant growth prospects, at a price that does not take account of the full value of the business. A really good business will still find investors, but the owner may have to re-assess his or her estimation of value.

- Sectors come in and out of fashion: 2001 was a good year for oil stocks, for example, and retail stocks have performed well early in 2002, with companies posting strong sets of figures driven by buoyant consumer spending. There is considerable investor interest in smaller natural resource companies, and demand continues for quality businesses providing outsourcing and other support services, particularly when underpinned by long-term contracts.

- Computing power continues to grow exponentially, and exciting discoveries are being made in biotechnology, materials sciences, information technology, electronics and energy generation. These developments will result in new products and businesses needing to be funded.
- The Internet is changing the way we do business; however, it is 'old economy' companies that are using it ever more effectively to market their products, communicate internally, streamline their procurement processes and cut the costs of distribution. On the other hand the Internet is increasing price transparency and putting pressure on margins. Companies that can balance these two conflicting forces will thrive, as will companies that become crucial to this method of communication. The market is looking for such businesses.
- Identifying the sector likeliest to do well is extremely difficult. Possible candidates are sectors where companies are well placed to benefit from expenditure by an ageing and increasingly wealthy population, and are able to offer environmentally sustainable solutions to energy, manufacturing and distribution problems. As well as companies with interesting new technologies, there will always be individual companies, even in unfashionable sectors, that can buck the trend and create exceptional value for their shareholders.
- Asset based businesses – property, for example – are valued at below their underlying asset value, encouraging managers to take these companies private. Private equity to fund these buy-outs will find its way to investors who will in turn have to find new businesses or assets in which to invest.
- On the other hand, as the population gets older, the amount of money that is taken out of pension funds to purchase annuities may eventually exceed the amount invested. When that happens pension funds may find themselves selling more shares than they buy, which would reduce interest in IPOs and put pressure on share prices. Pension funds may also choose to switch from equities to bonds, as the Boots pension fund has done, in order to secure a more certain income stream.

- The market for shares is polarizing. While AiM has become increasingly acceptable as a market for fund managers to invest in – indeed there are specialist funds, such as VCTs, that will invest predominantly or exclusively in AiM companies – those fund managers are looking to increase the size of company in which they invest. Europe is likely to follow the United States, where there are a diminishing number of funds that will consider investing in 'smaller' quoted companies, by which they mean companies with a market capitalization of less than $1,000 million. Already, many consider that a UK company with a market capitalization of less than £100 million should be quoted on AiM rather than the Full List. Except for the very largest companies, businesses seeking to float will increasingly look at AiM.
- In the first half of 2002, for the first time more companies transferred from the Full List to AiM than in the other direction. Companies used to see AiM as a market that would be a step prior to their moving 'up' to the Full List. Movement between markets is now seen as being 'across' – from one to the other. This perception is reflected in the additional regulatory requirements introduced in March 2002 for companies wishing to move from the Full List to AiM.
- Consolidation has been taking place in most sectors, creating giant companies that dominate their sector. The acquisition of Mannesman by Vodafone, the takeover of Natwest by Royal Bank of Scotland, the merger of Glaxo and Smith Kline and of BP and Amoco for example, have concentrated value in their particular sectors in fewer and fewer companies. Fund managers looking to achieve a spread of investments in a particular sector are increasingly obliged to think in pan-European or even global terms. Exchanges themselves are becoming integrated, and the likely outcome is that institutional investor interest will focus mainly on giant pan-European companies quoted on pan-European exchanges.
- Small, early stage companies cannot generally consider a flotation on the Full List. However, the size of business that floats on AiM is likely to increase, as larger companies, no

longer big enough for the Full List, apply for admission. Some businesses will be also attracted to AiM by tax advantages and by the lower cost of admission. Smaller companies already on the Full List are considering transferring across to AiM to take advantage of better coverage in investment publications and by brokers and analysts, different rules for announcing and approving transactions and lower ongoing costs. AiM no longer sees itself as a 'junior' market, and most institutions are interested in the size and sector of company rather than the stock market on which its shares are traded.

- International businesses are being wooed successfully – by the end of March 2002 AiM had admitted 42 overseas companies (making up almost 7 per cent of the total). It is hard to see another market eclipsing AiM as *the* market for smaller companies, both British and foreign. There are, however, no signs yet of AiM becoming part of a pan-European smaller companies market.

CONCLUSION

A company looking to float in 2002 has a realistic chance of success, provided that it has growth prospects and/or represents good value to investors. Those investors will probably not expect to see the sort of capital growth enjoyed during the bull market, and will place greater emphasis on yield. The quality of the company's earnings stream will therefore be particularly important.

There are sectors, for example in biotech or natural resources, where investors will fund a pre-profit business, or even an idea. For this to happen, both the idea and the people behind it must be exceptionally good. For most businesses however, the traditional virtues remain paramount – strong management, control of a market or a niche, and a unique selling proposition. And such a company, seeking to benefit from the funding and the advantages that a quotation offers, is increasingly likely to consider floating on AiM.

Notes

1. All items excluding mortgage interest payments. Source: Office of National Statistics Web site.
2. Based on the FTSE-100.
3. New companies raising money on the Full List. Source: London Stock Exchange.
4. From January 1988 to December 1999.
5. GDP seasonally adjusted, constant 1995 prices. Source: Office of National Statistics.
6. Based on the FTSE-30. Source: Office of National Statistics.
7. Source: WTRG Economics, www.wtrg.com.
8. Spending on recreation and culture. Source: Office of National Statistics.
9. Market value of pension funds. Source: Office of National Statistics.

2

Necessary and sufficient conditions for flotation

Colin Aaronson (Grant Thornton)

SUMMARY

- The formal criteria for admission are set out in Listing Rules and AiM Rules.
- For Full List companies, the UK Listing Authority approves admission to the Official List, and the London Stock Exchange approves admission to trading. However, a company must first satisfy its sponsor that it is suitable for admission.
- For AiM companies, the nomad (nominated adviser) has the formal responsibility of deciding if a company is suitable for admission. However, the London Stock Exchange has powers that can effectively prevent admission.
- For a flotation to be worthwhile, there must be sufficient trading in the shares so that there is a market in the stock.
- AiM has rules that relate specifically to start-ups.

- There are a number of practical considerations for overseas companies.

INTRODUCTION

If conditions are suitable for raising money in the City, and the company and its directors believe they are ready for life on a public market, they will need to approach an adviser who can guide them through the flotation process. That adviser will be a 'sponsor' if the company wants to have its shares quoted on the Full List (strictly speaking, the Official List of the United Kingdom Listing Authority – UKLA), or a 'nominated adviser' if it wants its securities to be admitted to trading on AiM. The company's auditors and accountants should know a suitable adviser. In addition, the Financial Services Authority has a list of sponsors, and the London Stock Exchange has a list of nominated advisers.

The adviser will confirm whether the company satisfies the criteria for admission laid down in the Listing Rules of the UKLA or the Rules of AiM; that is the easy part. The adviser must also decide if the company is, in its opinion, suitable for admission. This can be highly subjective, and will call for all the skill and experience at its disposal.

FORMAL CRITERIA FOR ADMISSION

The Listing Rules set out the criteria a company must satisfy for it to be eligible for admission to the Full List. The AiM Rules contain the equivalent rules for AiM. These criteria are shown in Table 2.1.

Legal status

A company must be incorporated under the relevant laws of the country of incorporation in a form that allows it to issue shares to the public. For UK companies that means being a plc.

Table 2.1 *Criteria for admission to the Full List and AiM*

Criteria	Full List	AiM
Legal status	Public limited company	Public limited company
Advisers	Must have a sponsor	Must have a nominated adviser and a broker
Minimum financial track record	3 years	No minimum
Minimum track record of management within a business	Appropriate expertise and experience	No minimum
Minimum aggregate share value at flotation	£700,000	No minimum
Minimum proportion if shares in public hands	25%	No minimum
Minimum working capital	At least 12 months	At least 12 months

Track record

A start-up business may apply for admission to AiM. The main consideration is that its proposed business is clearly defined, and that an investment company describes clearly its investment strategy.

A company considering admission to the Full List must have at least three years of audited accounts, and have carried on the same business for at least three years. A company that has been in existence for many years, but which changed its main activity less than three years before the proposed date of admission is not eligible. The accounts must have been drawn up in accordance with acceptable accounting standards (such as UK, US or International GAAP) and the audit report must usually be unqualified.

There are exceptions for mineral companies and scientific research based companies, as well as for innovative high growth companies. For other types of business, the UKLA also has the authority to waive these requirements.

Share valuation on admission

The formal minimum requirements for admission – for a Full List company it is £700,000 – are for practical purposes irrelevant. A sponsor or nominated adviser will not consider a company suitable for admission unless the market capitalization is large enough for the company to be of interest to investors.

The key investors are the institutions – fund managers – whose funds are increasing in size, and for whom $1 billion is regarded as a minimum desirable size of fund. With funds of this magnitude, it is not possible to make a sizeable investment in a company unless that company is itself significant.

In the UK, less than £1 billion market cap is coming to be regarded by the institutions as 'small cap', and below £100 million as 'microcap'. Today, there are some who argue that microcaps are no longer suitable for the Full List.

Shareholding in public hands

In this instance, 'public' means people or organizations other than directors of the company and its subsidiaries and persons connected to them, trustees of share schemes and pension funds set up for the benefit of directors and employees, anyone with authority to nominate a director, and shareholders with more than 5 per cent of any class of equity. Since directors and substantial shareholders are subject to dealing restrictions and are expected to hold their shares for the long term, they cannot really be said to be part of the market. The reason for setting a minimum percentage in public hands is to ensure that there is an active, or 'liquid' market in the company's shares. Twenty-five per cent is an arbitrary number – 10 per cent of a very large company may be a much more liquid market than 25 per cent of a very small one. Accordingly a percentage lower than 25 per cent may be acceptable if the market will work properly at a lower percentage.

A number of factors determine liquidity: the size of the company, the number of shares in public hands and the volume of trade in the shares. The greater the liquidity, the easier it is to sell large numbers of shares at the price quoted on dealers' screens. Liquidity in the stock can be measured by the bid-offer spread (the difference between the price at which shares can be bought and sold). At the end of April 2002, expressed as a percentage of the mid-market share price, Marks & Spencer with a market capitalization of £9 billion had a spread of 0.4 per cent. By way of comparison there were AiM companies with a market capitalization of around £1 million and a spread of 50 per cent. Small companies with an illiquid market in their shares will tend to have a much larger spread.

In order to ensure there is a sufficiently liquid market in the company's shares, brokers will sometimes place more shares than the company needs to satisfy its working capital requirements and its growth and acquisition strategy. Brokers will also sometimes ask owners to make available part of their shareholding to ensure that the market is adequately supplied with stock.

Investors prefer management not to have an interest greater than 50 per cent in a company. A larger shareholding reduces or removes the possibility of a hostile bid for the company succeeding, thereby reducing investors' potential upside, and aggravates the concern that dividend policy will be determined by the directors' personal tax position. The latter point can be dealt with by specifying the company's dividend policy in the admission document. In any event, large shareholdings are often unavoidable.

Working capital

Perhaps the single most important statement made in an admission document is the statement that the company has, in its directors' opinion, sufficient working capital for at least 12 months from the date of admission. Such is the importance of this statement that accountants will review working capital forecasts and confirm whether, in their opinion, the statement has been made after 'due and careful enquiry'.

For most companies with an existing business, this means ensuring that the forecasts are sufficiently robust to cope with any adverse events or a downturn in trade. For a pre-revenue business (a start-up), there should be sufficient working capital to continue operating at anticipated levels even if there are no sales at all.

The minimum amount that must be raised as part of the IPO will be determined by this requirement.

SUITABILITY FOR ADMISSION

A company may satisfy the minimum entry requirements, but it may still not be suitable for admission. Deciding on suitability is primarily the responsibility of a company's sponsor or nomad. Advisers will consider the following type of questions before taking a view:

- Is the company operating in a market that is growing, or at least not in terminal decline?
- Is the company itself likely to grow?
- Is there a high quality management team with no obvious weaknesses in any one particular area?
- Do the directors (and any controlling or influential shareholders) have the experience to run a public company, and can they demonstrate their integrity and financial probity?
- Have adequate measures been taken to ensure that there is proper corporate governance?
- Have suitable non-executive directors been appointed?
- Is there any unresolved litigation or other matter that could result in a significant liability to the business?

For an adviser the reputation and integrity of the market should be paramount. Only if it is confident that the company it is floating will enhance the reputation of the market and has a realistic chance of delivering real value to shareholders, should it proceed with a flotation. Ultimately it must ask, 'Do we really want to be associated with this company?'

CAN A COMPANY DELIVER VALUE?

Advisers may not wish to invest in a particular business even if they are bringing it to the market. They may, for example, be particularly risk averse; their responsibility is to ensure that the Listing Particulars or AiM admission document adequately describes those risks. The broker will have analysts who have a detailed knowledge of the industry, and will only be able to raise money from its institutional and private clients if they believe that the company is a good investment, even to the point of being willing to invest themselves.

Irrespective, adviser and broker must both believe that the business is fundamentally sound. Crucially, they must believe in the company's management.

Management

A company will be judged above all on the quality of its management. Commercial success would suggest that the managers are capable, but they could be running an under-performing company in a successful sector. It is therefore important to benchmark the company against other companies in the sector. Management can also be reacting to events rather than driving the business forward. Erratic or declining profits should ring alarm bells. And sometimes management just gets lucky for a while.

Some measures are objective, or at least obvious. A strong management team has the following characteristics:

- a clearly defined structure;
- a clearly identified leader;
- a breadth of skills encompassing finance, operations, marketing and sales. Operations include procurement, human resources, production and distribution. A capable finance director is key;
- demonstrable relevant experience;
- the ability to work as a team. A strong managing director should be surrounded by colleagues who have the ability to stand up to him or her. Although this judgement is subjective, it may well be the subject of due diligence;

- management information should be accurate, reliable and comprehensive, and delivered in a timely manner. If it is not, management cannot be said to have the systems necessary to run the business;
- accounting policies selected by management should err on the conservative, and be consistently applied;
- strong non-executive directors who are experienced in the ways of the City, and have the ability to impose proper public company practices on their colleagues.

Ultimately, assessment of management is highly subjective. Everyone has their own way of judging management – here are some things advisers tend to look for:

- a strong proactive leader, passionate about the business;
- the ability to answer questions, particularly on markets, competition and developments in their sector. It is particularly important that they understand and can explain the reasons for their success, and how that success can be built upon;
- an attitude of quiet confidence or cautious enthusiasm, grounded in reality;
- an air of calm. Directors who deal regularly with phone calls during meetings, or who cannot turn up on time, are disorganized (or possibly discourteous). Directors must be able to deal with strategic matters, and the business must be able to run itself during their absence. If it cannot, underlying management is probably inadequate;
- managers who do what they say they will do. If they do not, should investors trust them to deliver on their promises?

Irrespective of their ability, managers cannot make a silk purse out of a sow's ear, and if the underlying business model is fundamentally flawed, no manager will make it work.

The nature of the business

Different sectors come in and out of favour; unless the sector is in steep decline however, it may still be worth investing in. What is important is a company's position within a sector.

Management needs to be able to control the business if it is to drive it forward. An insignificant player in a market is subject to forces beyond its control. For that reason, successful companies like General Electric aim to be either first or second in every market in which they operate. An alternative strategy is to control a niche or segment of a larger market.

The company should not be over-reliant on one product. There should be a family of products and services, and a pipeline of new products under development. There should either be sufficient goodwill in the brand such that the company can charge a premium for its products, or the company should be a really efficient operator in a commodity market.

With very rare exceptions, the company should not be reliant on one, or even a very small number of customers (whose businesses can decline and whose management can change).

Certain products, components and services may be available from only a few suppliers, or even from one alone. While this is outside of management's control, management should have the ability to switch to alternative suppliers, or change components. It is crucial that the company being considered for flotation can continue trading if a key supplier halts delivery.

Ultimately, however, the facts speak for themselves, and management will be judged by its performance. Its track record in delivering value to investors must be measured and assessed.

Measuring success

Investors are looking for growth in earnings; the most popular measure of a company's performance therefore is earnings per share (EPS), which is simply post-tax profit divided by the number of shares. Since companies can increase profits by acquiring other businesses, the company can only be said to have a successful strategy and the ability to deliver growth in earnings if the amount of profit available to each individual shareholder has increased.

The earnings on which EPS is calculated are post-tax profit, not EBITDA (earnings before interest, taxation, depreciation and amortization), a measure that is commonly quoted these days. EBITDA focuses on the operating performance of the business. However, it does not take account of capitalized expenses that are subsequently amortized, and can therefore be highly misleading.

Even if a company is capable of delivering growth in earnings, it may still not be worth investing in. Earnings per share growth may in fact only represent a constant or even diminishing return on growing assets. A company whose only asset is cash and whose only activity is to earn and re-invest interest, will increase its earnings per share, but its return on assets or capital employed remains constant. Investors in such a company might prefer to invest the money in their own bank account. Management's ability should therefore be judged not only on its ability to grow EPS, but also by the company's return on capital employed (ROCE).

ROCE itself should be treated with a degree of caution, since earnings can be inflated in the short term by capitalizing expenses, and by aggressive stock valuation. ROCE depends on both its numerator (profit) and its denominator (capital employed). Asset valuation depends on the accounting policies selected, and the valuation of brands and other goodwill is particularly difficult. In theory, the market takes account of this in its share price. Ultimately it is (long-term) cash generation as a percentage of capital employed that is the yardstick by which performance should be judged.

SOME THOUGHTS ON OVERSEAS COMPANIES

Overseas companies are warmly welcomed on the London Stock Exchange. The criteria for admission are the same as for UK companies, and in the same way that a UK company must be a public limited company, an overseas company must be properly incorporated according to the laws of its country of incorporation, and it must be allowed by those laws to offer shares to the public. There are also a number of practical considerations that apply:

- Institutional investors like to hold and transfer their shares in dematerialized form (ie without a share certificate), using the CREST system. If overseas companies are to attract institutional investment, the laws of their country must allow shares to be held in dematerialized form.
- Investors will question why an overseas company is looking to float in London. Where the company comes from a country with a well-developed capital market (such as the United States, France or Germany), the concern is that the company is coming to London because it cannot raise the funds at home. Where countries do not have well-developed capital markets, this is less of a concern.
- It is generally accepted that an overseas business that is purely local, such as a chain of retailers operating exclusively in its own country, is not usually suitable for admission. The company's operations and activities must have an international dimension.
- Floating an overseas company is more expensive than floating its UK equivalent, particularly as the due diligence takes on an international dimension. Managing dual listings is an additional complication, and managing the release of information to markets in two time zones can be difficult.

The number of overseas companies is increasing, and advisers are becoming more skilled at handling cross-border transactions, even at the smaller company level. This trend looks set to continue as European large cap markets converge, and AiM continues to attract smaller companies by its efficient and pragmatic approach.

CONCLUSION

People invest in management, and management will be judged on results. Unless a company is able to deliver a return on assets that regularly exceeds the alternatives, its management cannot be said to demonstrate the skill that deserves investor support.

Advisers must ask themselves if they believe in the management team, and whether the company has a realistic chance of increasing value for investors. If they cannot answer in the affirmative, they should not introduce the company to the market.

Ultimately then, it is up to the owners of the business to convince their advisers that the company is suitable for flotation. But before they can do that, they must be sure in their own minds that flotation is suitable for them.

3

Finding the right financial strategy

Colin Aaronson (Grant Thornton)

SUMMARY

- Owners consider floating their companies for a variety of reasons:
    - to buy other businesses using tradable paper;
    - to help attract and incentivize staff whose share options are more valuable if the shares are quoted;
    - to value the company for taxation or estate valuation purposes;
    - to provide an exit route;
    - to raise finance.
- The costs and disadvantages of going public can outweigh the benefits. The owner must decide if these costs are acceptable.
- The key is to find a solution that satisfies the aspirations of business owners.

THE ADVANTAGES OF FLOTATION

Company owners consider going public for a number of reasons:

- There are considerable amounts of money available for flotation. In 2001, for example, £23 billion was raised on the Full List (excluding Eurobond issues) and AiM combined.
- It is common for quoted companies to raise funds after an IPO by way of a rights issue or placing. Provided that the company has performed as expected, and that the need for additional finance was either envisaged at the time of flotation or has resulted from better than expected trading, going back to the market for a second or subsequent round is perfectly acceptable. It is even acceptable in a rescue situation, as long as there are extremely good reasons for the company's difficulties.
- There are significant costs attached to other forms of funding. Private equity probably has a higher cost, to reflect both high rates of return demanded by the venture capital industry and the fact that the investor has to wait to realize his or her investment. An investment in a publicly quoted company may not be an exit for management, but for outside investors, depending on the liquidity of the market in the stock, an exit remains possible.
- Loan finance may appear to be cheaper than equity, but gearing a company increases its perceived risk and increases its cost of capital accordingly. In any case, loan finance may be neither appropriate nor available.
- Although owners of private companies should not regard an IPO as a means of exit, it may be possible to sell a proportion of their shares, and even all of them over time. A partial exit or an exit in stages could be very attractive if a trade sale is neither practical nor possible.
- A number of companies that rely heavily on the commitment of their staff – for example recruitment businesses or software developers – choose to go public as a means of incentivizing their employees. A carefully constructed share incentive

programme will be considerably more valuable if those shares can be traded.

- It may be easier to attract high quality staff to a publicly quoted company, when share options are available.
- Whilst the owner of a private business would not typically accept unquoted paper for his or her business, and quoted paper in an illiquid stock would be a distinct second best to cash, private vendors do accept shares, even if sometimes it is only part of the consideration.
- When either a trade sale, or an MBI candidate and funder are not available, the only exit might be a flotation as a means of bringing in new management.
- A quotation gives a formal valuation to a stock. This can be particularly useful for taxation purposes or for valuing an estate.
- Although it is easy to be cynical about profile raising and the perception of some public companies, the flotation process does raise public awareness of a business and commercially that can be very positive. There are also areas where a publicly quoted company will be at an advantage to a private organization when competing for contracts. Paradoxically, this applies to parts of the public sector.
- Going public raises a company's profile in the financial community; a public company can expect to receive offers of deals that would not be available to private businesses.

Whatever the reason or combination of reasons, the company's owners must understand why they want to float their company, and be fully aware of the consequent costs and disadvantages.

THE COSTS AND DISADVANTAGES OF FLOTATION

Flotation costs

The cost of bringing a company to market can be considerable. For a trading business intending to float on AiM, professional fees, excluding brokers' commissions of up to 5 per cent on funds raised, will start in the region of £250,000. For a trading company raising £5 million, that entails a total cost of £500,000. The professional fees for an admission to the Official List tend to be considerably higher.

A company embarks on the flotation process with no certainty that funds will be raised and admission achieved. True, some broking firms will 'underwrite' an issue, but that happens late in the process and most will only underwrite once the minimum amount required to be raised has already been committed. A proportion of the professional fees will be payable whether or not the flotation is successful.

Ongoing costs

Even if the flotation is successful, there are significant ongoing costs. An AiM company is obliged to retain a nominated adviser and a broker at all times. A publicly quoted trading company in the UK should have at least two non-executive directors, each of whom will be paid a retainer of at least £10,000 per annum. Registrars will be employed to maintain the share register, stock exchange membership fees have to be paid, interim and annual accounts have to be printed and posted to shareholders, financial PR companies employed and announcements made through a recognized information provider that will charge for its services. And a quoted company can expect to see its audit fees and legal bills go up. A small trading company should expect to see at least £100,000 come out of its bottom line profit.

The hidden cost of time

Directors and executives will have to spend a considerable amount of time both before and after flotation. During the run-up to admission, the directors are going to spend many hours with lawyers and accountants drafting prospectuses and admission documents, verifying each and every statement that appears in the document, being groomed for presentation to investors, rehearsing presentations, meeting broker sales teams and, finally, meeting investors. While all this is going on, the directors still have a business to run, and that business may suffer from their reduced involvement. As one nomad warns clients, 'You will be spending 24 hours a day on the flotation and running the business in your spare time.'

Once the company is on the market, the extra workload diminishes but does not disappear. Certain information must be released to the market – for example directors' share dealings or dealings by substantial shareholders, interim financial statements and final results – but the directors have an overriding obligation to ensure that the market is fully informed of all matters that would affect its perception of the company's value. Announcements have to be approved and released through the appropriate channels.

A private company can make do with a good accountant or financial controller. That same company, once public, will require a finance director who is not only commercially able, but also has the experience and personality to deal with the City.

These issues can be addressed, but they involve time and a cost that is difficult to estimate but is almost certain to be substantial.

Risk

For the directors, the whole process is not risk-free. Brokers will generally place shares with institutional and other clients, and will try to obtain the highest level of indemnities and warranties from the directors. The risk extends to the admission document – the directors must warrant that every statement is true and that nothing that would affect a reader's assessment of the company has been omitted.

LIFE IN THE PUBLIC DOMAIN

The company's broker will expect to meet the directors regularly, and brokers' analysts will subject the company to detailed scrutiny, both before and after flotation. If things are going well, it can be a very pleasant experience, but when results fail to meet expectations, the whole atmosphere becomes difficult and often extremely unpleasant. City folk have long memories, and do not usually give a second chance to someone who they feel has let them down. Moreover, all this happens in the public domain.

Selling a business to the public guarantees one thing – public awareness of your wealth. For most people, this is unwelcome publicity.

Restrictions on public company directors

Directors of a quoted company are subject to a number of obligations and restrictions on their freedom to act, which are known collectively as the rules of corporate governance. Regular board meetings will be held – usually monthly – agendas circulated and minutes prepared. Brokers and advisers will sometimes attend, and former owner-managers should expect to find themselves eclipsed at board meetings by their non-executive chairmen who will run the board.

The freedom that private companies enjoy – setting up share option schemes and establishing service contracts, for example – are constrained by what institutional investors consider acceptable practice. Relevant guidelines are set, for example, by the Association of British Insurers (the institutional investors' trade association), and failure to abide by them will reduce the number of investors who would consider investing in the company.

Qualifying the advantages of floating

The advantages that are often cited for going public must be qualified:

- Flotation is not an exit – investors will not invest if management is looking to sell. Owners looking for a complete exit would be better off considering a trade sale.
- Buying other companies with shares will depend on how attractive the vendor finds your own quoted paper. Even if a deal is available, shareholders may have to approve the acqui-

sition in a general meeting, and an announcement has to be made to the market.

- Going public can raise a company's profile, but the usual rules of business still apply: creditors and bankers are an increasingly canny and cynical lot, and a quotation will only help you raise other finance to a limited extent. Enron and Marconi were public companies – as were many dot coms – while some of the most profitable and best-known businesses are still private.
- Financial markets have become increasingly sophisticated, and there may be no need to raise equity finance from stock market investors.
- Substantial private equity is available from an extremely sophisticated and well-established venture capital industry. True, there are substantial costs attached, but investee companies can enjoy the advice and support of an experienced non-executive director introduced by its private equity provider and a venture capitalist whose advice many investee companies find extremely valuable.
- A number of types of debt finance are available.
- To cap it all, there may be significant tax disadvantages to going public.

The company's adviser should raise all these points, and perhaps others. Considering all the consequences of going public is an important part of preparing for flotation. The credibility of the company and its management will be enhanced if it can show that it has calculated the cost to the business in terms of time and money, and that given all that is involved, it still considers that the advantages outweigh the costs.

IDENTIFYING THE MOTIVATIONS OF THE OWNER-MANAGER

One of the most common characteristics of successful business-people is their passion for their business and the sheer amount of time they spend on it. For them, business success is more than a personal goal: it is a vital part of their life and intimately tied up with their self-esteem and sense of worth.

On the other hand there are many for whom business, whilst enjoyable, is a means to an end. Their company is often described as a 'lifestyle business'. There are many high quality businesses that are run in this way, but their owners are unlikely to have the drive and commitment for life on the public markets. For them, another solution is probably more appropriate.

There may be succession issues. If there is no obvious successor, and the owner is looking to retire, the company should consider preparing for a trade sale or an MBO. If the owner has other family members in the business, there are issues relating to roles, responsibilities and remuneration, which are usually more difficult to handle than when non-family members are involved. Estate and succession planning factors can exacerbate these problems. These issues need to be sorted out before a company can realistically consider flotation.

CONCLUSION

Anyone considering floating their company must weigh up carefully the costs and benefits of going public, and consider the available options in the light of their personal circumstances. An essential part of preparing for life as a quoted company is understanding and assessing these factors. Where family or succession issues are involved, it may be useful to enlist the help of a professional specializing in advising on these matters.

For those who decide that the costs of going public are too great, there are a number of alternatives, and these are discussed in the next chapter.

4

Alternative sources of finance

Colin Aaronson (Grant Thornton)

SUMMARY

- Owners consider floating their companies for a variety of reasons. The most common reason is to raise finance.
- An IPO rarely gives vendors an opportunity for an immediate exit, and there are more effective ways of achieving a disposal.
- The costs and disadvantages of going public can outweigh the benefits. The owner must decide if these costs are acceptable.
- There are other types of equity finance available, as well as debt finance that can supplement equity. For every business there is an ideal finance package, and for most companies this will not include an IPO.

INTRODUCTION

Companies come to the market for a number of reasons, but in most cases it is to raise finance. However, flotation may not be appropriate for the company in its present stage of development, or it may not be able to attract investor interest. Fortunately, other forms of finance are available.

For every company there exist a number of funding solutions involving different combinations of debt and equity. However, for companies that have been contemplating flotation, the main element of that package is likely to be equity.

EQUITY FINANCE

Private placing

A company can raise finance from outside investors without having to float the company. Situations in which this might happen are:

- Brokers and corporate finance boutiques may raise pre-IPO money, but this is predicated upon a subsequent IPO.
- Biotech and other high technology businesses can raise money from investors knowledgeable in their sector. If the technology proves successful, the rewards will be substantial whichever exit route is chosen.
- Companies may be given access to private investors who will invest without an IPO, although it is not common to raise money this way as investors have no obvious exit.

Investors will usually receive some sort of investment memorandum. The document will depend on the type of investor.

A sophisticated investor, such as an institutional fund manager, can invest on the basis of any document it chooses. A small group of investors (in simple terms, less than 50 people) can invest on the basis of a private placing memorandum. This is an investment advertisement, and as such must be approved by a person authorized under the Financial Service and Markets Act 2000. The person approving the document must ensure that the document is correct in all material respects and does not mislead the reader in any way whatever.

An offer to the public (which, in simple terms, is to more than 50 people) must be made in the form of a prospectus. The document must conform to The Public Offer of Securities Regulations 1995 (the POS Regs), a statutory instrument that defines an offer of securities to the public and specifies the form and content of a prospectus which must be published if such an offer is being made.

Private equity and venture capital

The venture capital industry is a great British success story. According to the British Venture Capital Association (BVCA), the UK venture capital, or private equity industry, is the largest in Europe, accounting for 28 per cent of private equity investment in 2001 and second in size only to the United States. The UK private equity industry has invested almost £50 billion (£35 billion in the UK) in over 23,000 companies since 1983[1]. Fifty per cent of private equity is used for expansion or development, the rest for management buy-outs and other transactions.

Venture capital (VC) is something of a misnomer. Although around 100 firms are listed by the BVCA as being interested in funding early stage businesses, both by inclination and by virtue of their preferred size of investment (over £5 million), most VC money is used to provide development capital or MBO finance. VCs will provide a mixture of debt and equity, calculated to earn them the desired rate return, which will tend to fall between 30 and 40 per cent per annum on an investment. This level of return is mainly achieved through growth, and is required to compensate the VC firm for the high degree of risk and the high level of resources it must commit to each investment. The greatest risk in any investment is that the VC will not be able to find a suitable exit route. It is estimated that the VC industry as a whole invested a net £10 billion in both 2000 and 2001, illustrating the difficulty it faces in exiting its investments.

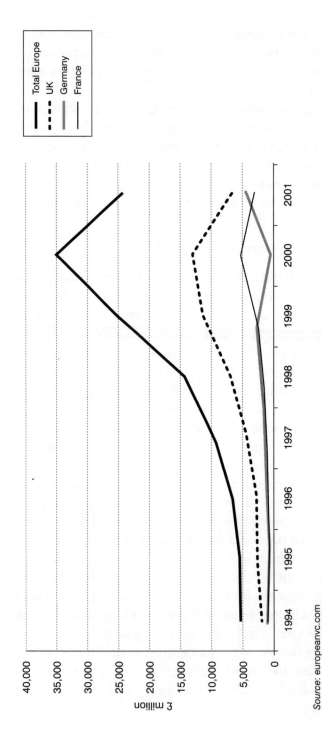

Source: europeanvc.com

Figure 4.1 *European private equity investment*

A company looking for private equity can identify potential investors by contacting the BVCA. Each VC firm has a stated set of investment criteria, based principally on industry sector, geographical location and stage of a company's development. A company should also consider appointing a financial adviser who will introduce it to a suitable VC firm. The adviser will know which VC firms are investing in a particular sector at any one time, and which are likely to be interested in funding that company. Using an adviser can save time, and should avoid the company unnecessarily hawking its business around the market. Indeed most VC firms either prefer or insist on dealing with an intermediary.

The first contact with a VC firm will be via a business plan, which should include detailed information on the company and financial forecasts. The VC will review the business plan and meet with management on several occasions before it decides to proceed with the due diligence as a pre-condition to investment in a business. It is estimated that no more than 2 per cent of business plans gain funding.

From the point at which the VC decides, in principle, to make an investment in a business to the point at which the company receives funds, there will be an average interval of three to four months. During that time, extensive due diligence is undertaken the cost of which will be borne by the company. This will involve accountants reporting on the operations of the business and on the integrity of the financial forecasts, industry experts reporting on the commercial operations of the business and on the assumptions underlying the financial forecasts, and lawyers reviewing contracts, questions of title to tangible assets and intellectual property and various other legal matters.

Some VCs become actively involved in their investee businesses, while others are more passive. Most will insist on a non-executive being appointed to the board. There is a cost to this involvement, but many companies welcome the experience and advice that these non-executives bring to the company.

Corporate venturing

Corporate venturing takes many forms, although in all cases a larger company provides funding or other support for a smaller company. At its most basic it can be a purely financial investment with a larger company taking an equity stake in a smaller company, usually in its own or in a connected industry. This is often done through a separate fund being set up specifically to invest in start-up and growth companies in the same way that a traditional venture capital firm would invest. The investment can also be indirect through other venture capital funds or trusts. Corporate venturing can also involve a tripartite arrangement with both a larger company and a VC firm investing in the business. The larger firm hopes to make a return on its investment when the company is sold or floats on a stock exchange. It may even acquire the investee business.

It can also be much more than purely financial. Some firms will offer a strategic alliance or support to smaller companies, helping them to develop products or services that will generate income or cost savings for both parties. This form of corporate venturing does not have to involve any equity participation or cash injection.

The concept of corporate venturing has existed for many years in the United States where traditionally corporate venturing has appealed to high growth sectors such as pharmaceutical or technology companies and where many of the top companies have a venture capital fund or offer strategic alliances. An investment in a smaller company may give the corporate venturer access to technology it does not own and which complements its own technology, or which could prove to be highly profitable in the future. As multinational companies become ever larger, their corporate culture and internal procedures make it more difficult for them to innovate. For such companies corporate venturing can give access to an accelerated product development programme and in a sense can even entail the outsourcing of innovation itself.

While the number of companies involved is much smaller in the UK, it has existed for many years and in many sectors. A government-sponsored initiative, under the auspices of the National Business Angels Network, was launched on 18 June 2002 to make corporate venturing more widespread in the UK. Tax advantages have recently been introduced: the 2000 Budget introduced a new tax incentive for companies wanting to invest in other trading companies. Under corporate venturing, if a company purchases shares in another company, 20 per cent of the amount invested can be set against its tax bill. The shares must then be held for three years, otherwise the relief is withdrawn. In order to qualify for this potentially valuable relief, there are various conditions that have to be satisfied and it is therefore important to structure the investment properly to ensure that the company receives the tax relief.

Business angels

Most companies considering a flotation will be looking for sums considerably in excess of those provided by business angels. For smaller businesses considering a flotation on AiM, they may occasionally be worth considering, particularly as a form of pre-IPO funding.

Business angels are successful and experienced businesspeople who want to become involved with a young growing business and have funds to invest. Business angels become actively involved in the companies they invest in, so being able to work with one is crucial to the success of the relationship. Research indicates that angels place greater emphasis on location than on industry sector, with most looking to invest in businesses located within an hour's drive from home.

Because of the confidential nature of the investment, it is only possible to approximate the size of the market. Research suggests that there are around 20,000 business angels in the UK, investing around £500 million a year in 3,500 businesses in amounts from £25,000 to £1 million, and occasionally more. Individually, angels rarely commit more than £50,000 to a single investment; amounts greater than that are usually provided by syndicates of angels.

It is a high risk, high reward activity; it is estimated that one-third of all investee companies fail, while around 20 per cent of all investee companies generate returns of greater than 50 per cent per annum for their angel investors.

The most common exit route for business angels, at 40 per cent, is some form of insolvency. Around half of all investments are sold either to other shareholders, management, a third party or to another business through a trade sale, and around 10 per cent through some form of flotation.

Most companies considering a flotation as a means of raising finance will be looking at larger amounts than £1 million. Such companies looking for private equity are therefore likely to be considering venture capital, rather than business angel finance.

DEBT FINANCE

It is tempting to consider debt as an alternative to equity, particularly with interest rates at their present level. However, debt has a hidden cost because it increases the company's risk. Debt finance may also not be available in the amounts that a company needs.

The following types of debt finance might be used to supplement equity or to reduce the amount of equity required.

Bank loans and overdrafts

The overdraft remains the most popular form of short-term funding. It is a flexible product designed for businesses with uneven cash flow, whose bank balance sometimes moves into the red.

The cheapest form of equity is retained profits, and a bank will quite reasonably expect a company to use its profits to pay back debt. If the company fails to generate profits, or convert those profits into cash, the bank may question its involvement with the business. Using profit to pay dividends simply emphasizes the need for personal guarantees.

Therefore, if the account is permanently overdrawn, and particularly if the facility is large relative to the company's assets and level of activity, the company cannot be regarded as adequately capitalized and the bank may well consider reassessing the basis on which it lends to the company. It may instruct independent accountants to report on the business, it may insist on converting the overdraft into some form of loan, or even insist on partial or total repayment.

Overdrafts should not be seen as additional funding, but as a product designed to give a level of financial flexibility.

Invoice discounting and factoring

Debtor based finance is estimated to account for around one-third of all short-term corporate lending, and is provided to approximately 30,000 businesses in the UK. Invoice discounting and factoring services are offered by a number of organizations, some of which are part of UK clearing banks, or by independent specialists. Most are members of the Factors & Discounters Association.

Factors (including, for the purposes of this discussion, invoice discounters) will lend against the value of their client's sales ledger, taking a charge over the sales ledger as security. As well as an absolute limit, they will set a percentage limit that will determine the amount available to lend to their client. The percentage figure will not exceed 90 per cent of the debtor book (it is usually well below that figure) and will depend on a number of things, including:

- the spread and quality of the sales ledger;
- the bad debt history;
- the level of goods returned from customers;
- the level of credit notes, end-of-year discounts and other retentions;
- the level of overseas debt;
- the terms and conditions of sale.

An example of an ideal customer for a factor would be an employment agency supplying staff to a number of high quality UK clients, whose terms and conditions of sale have been well prepared by its lawyers. Such a company will have a very low rate of retentions, and almost all its invoices will be paid in full. But there are many different types of business that use factoring services.

Once the percentage limit has been set, the company can borrow up to that percentage of outstanding sales ledger balances; funds are usually available promptly within a few days of an invoice being notified to the factor. As sales increase, funding available to the company will increase in line with the growing debtors book. Debtor based finance is therefore ideal for a growing business with a good sales ledger.

The factor will charge a rate of interest that depends on its assessment of the business, and an administration fee, to reflect the cost of monitoring its client's sales ledger.

Before a factor agrees to take on a client, it will undertake a detailed review of the company and its systems. It will need to be certain that the company is fundamentally sound and has the systems to provide the necessary information both to management and to its factor.

Under an invoice discounting service the company continues to administer its sales ledger and the service is usually undisclosed to customers. Factoring additionally provides a full sales ledger and collections service under which the factor takes on responsibility for the company's sales ledger. This carries an additional cost, but reduces the need for accounting staff within the company. Factoring used to have the reputation of being the last resort of a company unable to raise money elsewhere. Today, factoring is seen more as another type of outsourcing, providing businesses with a professionally run sales ledger.

Debtor based finance makes intelligent use of a company's sales ledger as the basis for calculating its facility and as the basis of its securities. Companies would do well to consider it where there is a strong debtors book with a low rate of retentions, the business is growing, and its working capital needs fluctuate in accordance with its sales activity.

Leasing

As a rule, businesses should not use short-term debt to finance long-term assets. Bankers like to match the term of the borrowing with the life of the asset. Leasing is a popular way of paying for cars, aircraft, ships, plant and machinery and other fixed assets, setting the life of the borrowing to match the life of the asset.

Leasing is provided by banks, merchant banks, finance house subsidiaries of banks and building societies, independent finance companies and the finance arms of manufacturers and retailers. Most leasing companies are members of the Finance & Leasing Association. The FLA estimates that its members are currently providing £110 billion of funding to business, including 28 per cent of UK fixed capital investment.

Leasing may be either on balance sheet (finance leases) or off balance sheet (operating leases). A finance lease is akin to borrowing money to purchase an asset. With a finance lease, substantially all the risks and rewards of ownership are transferred to a lessee, and this is reflected in its accounting treatment (the company is required to capitalize the asset and record the liability to pay lease rentals in its balance sheet). An operating lease is akin to renting an asset and the company using the assets will normally pay a monthly rental; the only accounting entries are the lease payments as they occur. Operating leases are suitable for assets such as cars and aircraft or indeed any asset where a residual value can be calculated. In either case the tax allowances will be used by the leasing company, which is the legal owner of the goods.

Interest rates will be linked to base rate or LIBOR, and can be either fixed or variable. Rentals can be set to match the company's cash flow, which is particularly useful if business is seasonal.

Like all the other forms of debt finance discussed so far, leasing may be used in conjunction with many other forms of funding.

Financing property

Trading companies do not consider a flotation in order to buy property, but sometimes part of the funds being sought is earmarked to purchase a building. Investors do not like their funds to be used to buy property (unless they are investing in a property company). If a company is considering a flotation, or any other form of equity fundraising, it should remove the cost of buildings from its funding requirement.

Renting a building or buying it with the help of a mortgage-backed loan are appropriate funding methods. It is also common practice for owners of a business to hold property in their pension fund and rent it to their company.

EXITING THE BUSINESS

Finance raised through a flotation should be used to develop the business or to replace debt; investors do not want their money used to pay off the owner. It may be possible for vendors to take a small proportion (generally less than 25 per cent) of the funds raised as cash for themselves, and it may be possible to offload the owners' shares over time, although brokers do not welcome the depressing effect of this 'overhang' on the share price. Brokers will sometimes ask owners to make shares available to 'feed the market' if there is sufficient unsatisfied investor demand. In most situations however, selling the business to a trade buyer or to an MBO team is a more appropriate solution.

Trade sale

A trade sale is the most straightforward option. The company could be a good strategic fit with another business, or could bring additional capacity and staff, technology and customers to a competitor. The prices paid by trade purchasers are likely to be greater than those paid by MBO teams, to reflect these synergies.

The price paid can be a fixed sum, or be a fixed sum plus an earn-out. An earn-out is additional performance-related consideration and will not usually form part of the overall consideration unless the vendor intends staying with the company post sale. With a fixed sum, the vendor can simply walk away.

Trade sales can be negotiated directly between vendor and purchaser, although this is more likely to happen when the purchaser makes the initial approach. Otherwise, the vendor will probably sell its company through a disposal specialist.

Selling a business is something most businesspeople do once in their lifetime. They have no experience of this type of transaction, and may well not have the personnel available to handle the details of the transaction; such people considering selling their businesses would do well to contact a disposal specialist. The specialist could be working within a corporate finance department of an accountancy firm, a small merchant bank or a corporate finance boutique. A disposal specialist will use his or her knowledge and resources to groom the company for sale, prepare a sale memorandum, identify potential buyers, approach a number of businesses, manage the bid process and negotiate with the eventual purchaser. The specialist will also project manage the sale process, drawing up a timetable, coordinating the professionals, and dealing with any ongoing negotiations.

Of course there is a fee for this service, usually a percentage of funds raised, which has to be weighed against the additional consideration that good professionals can earn for their client.

Mergers

Mergers are a variant on the trade sale theme, the difference being that a vendor receives shares instead of cash as his or her company is merged with another. This can actually make exiting more difficult as the vendor no longer has full control over his or her business.

However, there are circumstances where merging makes sense, including where there are obvious synergies and there is a feeling of trust between the vendors, and where the company's future on its own is uncertain.

Once a deal is agreed, both sides will conduct due diligence on the other, lawyers will draft sale and purchase agreements and advisers will project manage the process, arranging additional working capital as necessary. Merger and acquisition specialists are usually found in corporate finance teams within accountancy firms or specialist corporate finance businesses.

Management buy-outs and management buy-ins

It may not be possible to find a trade buyer. The owner of a company may also wish to reward his or her employees by allowing them to buy the business at a lower price than a trade buyer would be prepared to pay. When a company is sold by its owner to its incumbent management, the deal is known as a management buy-out or MBO.

A management buy-in, or MBI, differs in that the purchaser is an outside team that is 'parachuted in' to buy the business. Because the MBI team does not have the inside knowledge that a MBO team will have, it will generally be of a significantly higher calibre.

Sometimes an existing management team is supplemented by a particularly capable and experienced businessperson who is brought in from outside to lead the MBO team. This type of deal is referred to as a BIMBO.

An MBO or MBI team will appoint an adviser who will put together a financing package, which will probably comprise equity and mezzanine finance from a VC house, and bank or other debt. A VC will expect to see the same sorts of return as it would from the provision of development capital. The process is much the same.

WHEN THINGS GO WRONG

Companies run out of cash for a number of reasons. Sometimes it is possible to trade out of difficulties but often an injection of cash is needed. If the business model is fundamentally flawed, or the management incompetent, it will not be possible to raise fresh capital and some form of insolvency usually follows.

Where there are extenuating circumstances, it may be possible to come to an arrangement with creditors and even to raise additional finance. There are a number of funds that invest in turnaround situations. These funds will undertake rapid due diligence, and usually install managers to run the company.

Given the risky nature of this type of investment, the rewards from a turnaround that succeeds will be substantial.

Note

1. BVCA.co.uk, 3 September 2002

Part II

The flotation process

5

The regulatory framework

Martin Shaw (Pinsent Curtis Biddle)

INTRODUCTION – BASIC CHOICES

A company that is seeking to float and have its shares publicly traded has the choice of a variety of markets. The choice of market will be influenced by a range of factors, including the following:

- the level of regulation and/or the degree of disclosure required by a particular market;
- the entry requirements of a particular market;
- the profile of the companies listed on that market;
- access to potential investors; and
- the relevance of the market to the company's business.

The potential markets include the London Stock Exchange's main market for listed securities (coupled with a listing on the UK Listing Authority's Official List), AiM (also operated by the London Stock Exchange) and Easdaq (aimed at high growth companies with a market capitalization at admission of £30 million plus). Overseas choices include Easdaq's US cousin Nasdaq and the markets operated by continental exchanges such as EURO.NM and Der Neuer Markt. Each has its own rulebook and pool of typical investors.

For a significant UK company that falls outside the fairly limited scope of Easdaq, the primary choice is likely to be between a listing on the UKLA's Official List coupled with admission to trading on the London Stock Exchange's main market (referred to as a 'full listing') and a listing on AiM.

The London markets have many advantages for companies over the alternative European markets – in particular, a higher profile, a proven track record of attracting companies and investors, critical mass, a concentrated pool of investors in the Square Mile and investor confidence through being part of a well-regulated market.

LONDON STOCK EXCHANGE PLC

The London Stock Exchange (the LSE) is one of the world's oldest and largest stock exchanges. The main market comprises those securities admitted to the Official List by the Financial Services Authority (FSA) acting as the UK Listing Authority (UKLA) for the purposes of the Financial Services Markets Act 2000 and EC Directives. The listing of such securities is subject to the UKLA Listing Rules (often referred to as the Purple Book) and the LSE's own Admission and Disclosure Standards.

The LSE has introduced 'sub' markets within the main market: techMark, extraMark and AiM.

techMark

In November 1999, the LSE introduced techMark, to bring together both listed and new innovative technology companies, cutting across industrial sectors and size bands. techMark acts as a market within a market, rather than as a separate trading platform – grouping together companies from a wide range of FTSE industrial sectors into a market with its own identity and its own FTSE indices.

The introduction of techMark involved the creation of a new market segment for the techMark companies, the development of new indices that include only techMark companies and the preparation of a new Listing Rules chapter for innovative high growth companies that do not have a three-year track record (Chapter 25 of the UKLA Listing Rules).

The introduction of techMark was intended to have the following effects:

- investors to be able to target technology stocks with more ease, without having to pick through individual sectors;
- the pricing of technology stocks was to be more uniform; and
- new (and smaller) applicants to be seen alongside their more established and larger technology counterparts.

To date, techMark has been a great success and many existing listed companies and new applicants are keen to be included in the new index.

Application for listing under Chapter 25 of the UKLA Listing Rules and application for inclusion in techMark are two separate processes. The UKLA will make its own decision as to whether a particular company should be listed under Chapter 25. The decision as to whether to include a particular company in the techMark index will be a decision made by the LSE in consultation with a body of individuals within City institutions, known as the Technology Advisory Group.

extraMark

In 2000, the LSE created a new market called extraMark for innovative investment companies and products to provide investors with special investment opportunities.

AiM

AiM is the LSE's Alternative Investment Market and was launched in 1995. AiM is a separate and alternative London market for new or small companies.

AiM was developed to meet the needs of the smaller, growing companies that might not meet the full criteria for a listing on the main market or for whom a more flexible regulatory environment is more appropriate. The entry criteria for AiM make it possible to gain admission without a trading record, an established management team or any minimum market capitalizations.

AiM is not bound by the UK Listing Authorities' Listing Rules. The AiM companies benefit from a more flexible regulatory environment, which can act as a stepping stone to those that may aspire to the main market using a simplified admission process.

The AiM Rules cover *admission requirements*, such as the free transferability of shares, public company status and use of recognized accountancy standards. Unlike the UKLA Listing Rules, there is no minimum trading record or percentage of shares in public hands. The AiM Rules also cover *continuing obligations*: general disclosure obligations, changes in broad structure and transactions outside the ordinary course of business that are entered into by AiM companies. Unlike companies subject to UKLA Listing Rules, AiM companies do not need to obtain shareholder approval for transactions other than reverse takeovers and they do not have to state in their annual reports whether they have complied with the corporate governance recommendations.

However, because AiM companies are young companies, the AiM Rules provide that the companies must at all times have a nominated adviser and a nominated broker, and detailed histories of the directors are to be set out in the company's admission document and on any appointment of a director.

The choice between the main market and AiM is largely a question of the company's size and the stage in its cycle. Assuming the decision is taken to launch the IPO on the LSE, the company's advisers can advise whether the company is more suitable for listing on the main market or AiM.

LEGAL FRAMEWORK

The legal and regulatory issues in relation to the marketing of securities (principally a company's ordinary shares) in the UK are of course detailed and complex. Therefore the chapters of this book are restricted to considering regulatory issues relating to a full listing and a listing on AiM. They do not deal with the offer of securities by a private or foreign company, by a public company prior to its obtaining a listing (for example, to effect venture capital investment) or by a listed company where such securities are not themselves to be listed. The regulatory framework regarding the trading and transfer of already issued listed and unlisted securities is also outside the scope of this work.

The marketing of securities in the UK is regulated by the Financial Services and Markets Act 2000 (FSMA), which replaced the Financial Services Act 1986. The FSMA is being implemented by a significant amount of secondary legislation introduced during the second half of 2001. In very broad terms, shares may only be offered to the public (which has a much wider definition than might be expected) where they are 'listed' on the Official List or where the Public Offers of Securities Regulations 1995 (POS Regs) have been complied with (and with which the AiM Rules comply).

UKLA and the Listing Rules

The Financial Services Act confers powers on the Financial Services Authority (the FSA) to make and administer rules for the granting of 'listed' status to securities by admission to listing pursuant to Part IV of the Act and by their inclusion on the 'Official List'. The FSA, which is to be the new super-regulator for the financial services industry in the UK, operates through its division known as the United Kingdom Listing Authority, or UKLA, in relation to listed securities; its rules are known as the 'Listing Rules'. (This function was previously carried out, up to 1 May 2000, by the LSE under its Listing Rules, which were colloquially known as the 'Yellow Book'. The UKLA's Listing Rules are, in form and content, substantially the same as the old Yellow Book.)

A two-stage admission process applies to companies that want to have their securities admitted to the London Stock Exchange's market for listed securities. Application first needs to be made to the FSA, as the UK Listing Authority, for the relevant securities to be admitted to the Official List in compliance with the Listing Rules. Second, application needs to be made to the LSE for the relevant listed securities then to be admitted to trading on its market for listed securities as set out in its 'Admissions and Disclosure Standards' brochure.

It is only once both of these processes have been completed and admission to listing and to trading has become effective that the securities are officially listed on the LSE. It is a condition of the new Listing Rules that, to be listed, securities must be admitted to trading on the LSE.

AiM

AiM is operated as a 'regulated market' under the Act by London Stock Exchange plc, which has been formally designated as a 'recognized investment exchange' (and is therefore empowered to operate a regulated market) under the Act.

The rules of AiM in relation to admission are based in large part on the POS Regs. Once admitted to AiM, companies are required to comply with the Traded Securities (Disclosure) Regulations 1994 (which provide a statutory obligation to disclose unpublished price-sensitive information to the market) and the continuing obligation requirements under the AiM Rules.

Role of the LSE

Following the appointment of the FSA/UKLA as the 'competent authority', London Stock Exchange plc now has responsibility for admitting companies and their listed securities to trading on the market for listed securities operated by the LSE. The LSE will also continue to operate and regulate AiM, which is not affected by the transfer to the FSA.

The LSE is currently the only operator of a market in listed securities in the UK, but the segregation of its role as 'competent authority' and 'market operator' recognizes that other markets for listed securities in the UK, such as Nasdaq Europe, could be created in competition.

Status of the Listing Rules and AiM Rules

It is worth noting that neither the Listing Rules nor the AiM Rules constitute 'laws' as such, and breach of them does not of itself constitute a criminal offence. A breach of these Rules can, though, still have serious commercial consequences for a company and its directors involved, and these are examined in greater detail in the next chapter.

ADMISSION CRITERIA

Official List

The main regulatory requirements a company must meet to obtain a full listing are as follows:

- *Incorporation*: there must have been a formal incorporation as a distinct legal entity under the laws of the appropriate jurisdiction – in the case of a UK company, this means that plc status will have been obtained.
- *Accounts and trading*: the company must have three years' accounts audited to a period ending no more than three months before the float, which demonstrate trading and revenue earning during that period.
- *Directors*: the company's directors and senior management must be able to demonstrate the right level of skills and experience to run the business and must be free of any conflict of interest which could interfere with this.
- *Working capital*: the company must demonstrate, backed up by an accountants' report, that it has sufficient working capital for current needs and for the next 12 months.
- *Independence from controlling shareholders*: the company must be able to carry on its business independently from any share-

holder owning 30 per cent or more of the shares or who controls the majority of the votes at board level.

- *Public holding of shares*: at least 25 per cent of the company's shares shall be held by the public (which excludes the directors, related pension funds or employee share schemes and anyone with a right to nominate a director or with a 5 per cent interest or more in shares).
- *Market capitalization*: the minimum acceptable market capitalization is £700,000 (although in practice, it will have to be substantially higher for the float to be economically viable).

The requirements for a 'track record' have recently been relaxed to allow 'innovative high growth' companies to obtain a full listing if at least £20 million is being raised where it can be demonstrated that funds can be obtained from 'sophisticated investors' and also provided certain other criteria are met in terms of information to be included in the prospectus and continuing obligations (including quarterly financial reporting).

A company seeking a full listing must engage a sponsor/listing agent whose identity is acceptable to the UKLA, which must supervise the application process and confirm suitability of the applicant to the UKLA.

Assuming these conditions are in place, the company can then proceed to prepare a prospectus or listing particulars required for the listing to take effect, providing the very detailed information specified in the Rules about the company, its business, management, capital structure and ownership and the shares being listed.

AiM

AiM is marketed as 'The London Stock Exchange's public market for small, young and growing companies' and, as such, its application criteria and continuing obligations are more relaxed than for the Official List (making it potentially much less attractive for certain sorts of investor).

The principal admission requirements are:

- incorporation as a plc (for a UK company);
- the appointment of a nominated adviser and nominated broker (equivalent in many respects to a sponsor on the Official List);
- the prior publication of at least one set of audited accounts;
- shares that are freely transferable.

Where a company has been generating revenue for less than two years, directors and all employees who hold an interest of 1 per cent or more in the company's shares must agree not to sell any interests they may have in those shares for at least one year from joining AiM.

Having fulfilled these requirements, a company may proceed to prepare its prospectus in accordance with the AiM Rules, with the more limited information to be included than for a full listing.

Having 'floated' and achieved a listing on the Official List or AiM, a company will then have to ensure that it complies with the 'continuing obligations' under the rulebooks; these are examined in Part III.

6

Alternative stock exchanges

Colin Aaronson (Grant Thornton)

SUMMARY

- As one of the most important capital markets in the world, there is practically no company or no fundraising too large for the London Stock Exchange.
- For smaller companies wanting a quotation, but which are neither ready nor willing to bear the cost of a flotation, there are alternatives.
- It is hard to find a reason for going elsewhere; information requirements on Nasdaq illustrate why increasing numbers of US companies are considering transferring their listings to London.

INTRODUCTION

London has one of the largest and most sophisticated capital markets in the world, and provides a stock market for some of its largest companies. Given the substantial funds available and the convenience of a local market, it is not common for a UK company to list anywhere other than London.

However, during the second half of the 1990s, and particularly during the few years before the collapse of the TMT sector, 'technology' companies from around the world sought to float on Nasdaq, including ambitious UK technology companies that saw AiM as a stepping stone to that market. The decline in technology stocks since the spring of 2000, on Nasdaq and elsewhere, has made it increasingly difficult to raise money for young technology businesses. Combined with the success of AiM, this has meant that considerably fewer UK companies see Nasdaq as a viable alternative to London. This realization may have contributed to Nasdaq's decision to acquire Easdaq, a Belgium based pan-European exchange.

As discussed elsewhere in this book, institutional investors are increasingly thinking in pan-European terms and national markets are combining to reflect this trend. Euronext is the result of the mergers of the French, Dutch and Belgian markets, and the London Stock Exchange is still seen by some as a potential merger partner for the Deutsche Borse in spite of the abortive merger negotiations in 2000. These markets will be competing for business and, for larger companies operating across Europe, a flotation overseas may be attractive.

There are also alternatives for smaller companies wanting a quotation. The Full List or even AiM may not be appropriate, or the costs of listing may simply be judged unacceptable or unnecessary. For such companies, the main alternative is OFEX.

OFEX

OFEX started trading in October 1995, operated initially by J P Jenkins Limited, a London based firm of stockbrokers. Since January 2002 the market has been operated by OFEX plc. At the end of May 2002, there were almost 200 securities trading on OFEX with a combined market cap of approximately £1.5 billion.

Membership of OFEX will enable a company seeking to raise its profile, or to obtain a visible share price calculated independently of the company itself, to achieve these goals without incurring the cost of a flotation on AiM or the Full List. To be sure, there are some substantial businesses whose shares are quoted on OFEX such as Weetabix Ltd with a market cap of approximately £300 million, but most OFEX companies are considerably smaller than companies quoted on AiM or the Full List. For such companies, OFEX enables shareholders to trade shares independently of the company itself.

As a matter of policy, most institutions will not invest in OFEX companies, but there are a significant number of private investors who are prepared to invest in a company provided its shares can be traded, and they are prepared to have those shares traded on OFEX.

Although OFEX is not a 'Recognized Investment Exchange' as defined by FSMA 2000, it is still a prescribed market for the purposes of section 118 of that Act, and FSMA's rules regarding market abuse apply to OFEX, just as they do to AiM and the Full List.

Shares on OFEX are not 'listed', which gives certain tax advantages that are also available to AiM companies but not to those on the Full List.

How shares are traded on OFEX

Investors buy and sell shares in OFEX companies by placing instructions with a stockbroker who is a member of OFEX. The broker will place an order with a market maker at J P Jenkins Limited. If there is a sufficiently liquid market in the stock, J P Jenkins will give a 'firm quote'. The quote will be a bid-offer spread, indicating the prices at which J P Jenkins will buy and sell the shares, as well as a 'size' – the number of shares it will trade at those prices. Trading in OFEX shares in this way is not markedly different from trading in shares on other markets.

Where there is an illiquid market in the stock, it may not be possible to effect a trade. In such circumstances, J P Jenkins will issue a 'basis' price, which is merely an indication based on recent experience. If investors place a buy or sell order in such a situation, they will have to wait until a seller or buyer appears before J P

Jenkins can match the two parties. This is referred to as a 'matched bargain'.

OFEX is sometimes incorrectly described as a 'matched bargain facility'. It does offer that facility, but only when there is not sufficient liquidity in the stock. As such it is a reflection of the size of some OFEX companies, rather than a description of the market itself.

Information about companies is disseminated by Newstrack, OFEX's news and information service. Price-sensitive information, as well as other material, is released via Newstrack to OFEX's own Website and to third party information providers such as Reuters. Share prices are shown on the Website, and are quoted, *inter alia*, in the *Financial Times.*

Joining OFEX

The decision on whether a company is to be admitted is taken by OFEX alone. Unlike AiM or the Full List, there is no requirement for an admission document or Listing Particulars (although a company raising funds will need to issue a prospectus or a private placing memorandum). Assuming the company is considered suitable for admission, it must provide the information required by the OFEX rules. These rules, which were updated in January 2002, require the following basic information to be provided:

- company information questionnaire;
- declaration by each director and proposed director of that person's business activities;
- admission agreement;
- copies of the Memorandum and Articles of Association of the company;
- copies of the annual report and accounts for the last three years (or since incorporation if later);
- additional information material to the analysis of the investment potential of the applicant company. This can include material trading agreements, agreements in respect of intellectual property and related party transactions;

- copies of any prospectuses or private placing memoranda issued during the period for which accounts have been presented to OFEX, up to the date of proposed admission to trading;
- a letter from the directors indicating their intentions regarding disposal of their shareholdings in the 12 months after admission;
- a letter from the directors confirming that they have adopted and will abide by the model code. (The model code is set out as an appendix to Chapter 16 of the Listing Rules of the UK Listing Authority, to which directors of listed companies must adhere in respect of dealing in their company's shares.); and
- a letter from the corporate adviser stating that its client has complied with the rules relating to admission.

A corporate adviser, who must be a member of OFEX, is required to submit the application. Overseas or 'start-up' companies (those that have not prepared three years of audited accounts), also need to retain a corporate adviser following admission. The detailed rules are set out in the OFEX rule book.

AiM or OFEX?

Floating on AiM is more expensive than joining OFEX, and the ongoing costs are generally higher. However, most institutional investors will not invest in OFEX companies, which means that there are larger funds available to companies on AiM.

The market for AiM shares is more liquid than for OFEX shares, but this is more a reflection of the size of companies that are attracted to it. OFEX may therefore be appropriate when a company wants a share-trading platform at a lower price than on AiM, or perhaps as its first venture into the public arena.

OFEX and AiM do not see each other as rivals. They are designed to satisfy different needs, and see themselves as being appropriate for different stages of a public company's life. OFEX is regarded by many as a good training ground for a small company starting life as a publicly quoted company, but with lower costs than AiM.

ShareMark®

ShareMark is operated by The Share Centre Ltd, which is a member of the London Stock Exchange and is regulated by the FSA. It is an electronic share auction market, matching buyers and sellers at a single price. It is intended to appeal to companies whose shares are infrequently traded, and the application process is designed to be as simple as possible. It is therefore likely to appeal to smaller businesses.

Share auctions take place periodically on pre-determined dates rather than continuously, with buyers and sellers placing orders online up to 2 pm on the day of the auction. ShareMark matches this supply and demand at an auction price determined by the orders received during the auction period. There is no bid-offer spread, just a price reached at auction. However, an indicative price is shown, which reflects buy and sell orders.

By the end of August 2002, there were six companies listed on ShareMark's Web site, including The Share Centre Ltd's parent company, Share plc. ShareMark is adopting the proven approach of Internet based auction houses and applying it to share trading. However, it remains to be seen if ShareMark becomes a realistic competitor to the other more established markets. It is difficult to predict whether ShareMark will become an effective medium for raising money, although it may be more successful as a low-cost trading facility.

OVERSEAS ALTERNATIVES

A UK company whose business is predominantly overseas or which is of particular interest to overseas investors, might consider listing overseas, either as a dual listing or even alone. For example, a number of AiM listed natural resource companies are quoted overseas as well as in London.

There are a number of reasons why a company might consider listing on a foreign market:

- to achieve a higher valuation;
- to provide easier access for local investors and achieve greater liquidity;
- to improve visibility within a particular market.

Given the size of the domestic capital market, UK companies seeking a listing overseas will almost certainly have investors question their motives, particularly if fundraising is involved. The only circumstances in which the company will be able to justify its decision to float overseas are if it has foreign investors, customers or suppliers.

A dual listing has all the advantages listed above, but it also has a number of disadvantages. These include:

- the extra time taken to travel overseas to meetings with analysts and investors;
- higher costs arising from the different listing requirements of both markets and the greater amount of compliance work that is required;
- announcements have to be timed with care to ensure that one market is not aware of a piece of price-sensitive information that has not been released to the other. This problem is most likely to occur when the two markets are in significantly distant time zones, such as Sydney and London;
- it may be necessary to produce accounts under two sets of accounting rules, and to publish information in two or more languages.

For a company that is prepared to bear the additional cost of floating overseas, and can benefit from the advantages such a listing offers, Europe has over 20 new markets created since 1995. They range in size from the Prague Stock Exchange New Market that opened in September 1999 and at August 2002 had yet to admit its first company, through AiM with over 600 companies and a market cap of €19 billion, to Euronext with over 1,600 companies and a market cap of approximately €2,000 billion.

Admission requirements

The four main growth markets that a UK company might consider are AiM, Nasdaq Europe, Neuer Markt, and the Nouveau Marche, which is part of Euronext.

Neuer Markt emerged as the European brand leader for technology stocks, although its reputation has been tarnished recently by reported failings of market regulation. AiM remains the leading European market for growth companies, although its companies are on average considerably smaller than on the other three exchanges. This is reflected in the respective sizes of each of these markets and their respective admission requirements, which are shown in Table 6.1 as at 31 December 2001.

The overall situation is likely to change, with one or more of these markets possibly merging with another. Consolidation of stock markets is likely to continue, being driven by a number of forces. These factors include:

- the increasing tendency of fund managers to think in pan-European terms;
- the de-mutualization of most European exchanges, allowing them to buy and sell each other's shares freely;
- the introduction of the Euro, which has made it easier to compare companies across borders;
- the requirement that all EU companies on a regulated market prepare consolidated accounts in accordance with International Accounting Standards (IAS) by 2005.

On 30 May 2001, the European Commission issued a proposal for a Directive that would make it mandatory to issue a prospectus when securities are offered to the public or when shares are admitted to trading. The objective of the Directive is to harmonize requirements across the EU, and it does go some way to addressing the cross-border complications of raising capital. However, it imposes higher and more expensive standards of disclosure, appropriate for larger companies, on smaller companies that presently enjoy simpler and less expensive

Table 6.1 *The four main growth markets for UK companies*

	AiM	Nasdaq Europe	Neuer Markt	Nouveau Marché
STATISTICS				
Established	1995	1996 (as Easdaq)	1997	1996
Number of companies	629	50	327	164
Of which foreign companies	42	39	55	11
Market cap	€19 billion	€8 billion	€50 billion	€15 billion
ADMISSION CRITERIA				
Total number of shares offered to the public	No minimum requirement	Minimum of 100 shareholders, minimum 20% in public hands	Aggregate nominal value of €0.25 million or 100,000 shares 25% free float (50% must be capital increase)	Minimum market value of €5.5 million; minimum of 20% in public hands (50% must be capital increase)
Initial equity required	No minimum requirement	Minimum €0–20 million depending on route to admission	Minimum of €1.5 million	Minimum of €1.5 million
Market capitalization	No minimum requirement	€0–50 million depending on route to admission	Minimum of €5 million	Minimum of €20 million
Previous trading history	No minimum requirement	0–2 years, depending on route to admission	Minimum of 3 years financial statements, although exceptions are possible	No historical minimum requirement, but a 3 year business plan is needed
Past profitability	No minimum requirement	€0–1 million depending on route to admission	No minimum requirement	No minimum requirement
Market makers	No minimum requirement	Minimum of 2	Minimum of 2 (designated sponsor)	Minimum of 1

Table 6.1 _contd_

	AiM	Nasdaq Europe	Neuer Markt	Nouveau Marché
Advisers	Nominated adviser, broker	Lead adviser and broker	1 bank or special financial institution	2 nominated advisers (one must be a lead adviser)
Reporting language	English	English	German and English	French
Accounting standards	UK GAAP, IAS or US GAAP	US GAAP or IAS	US GAAP or IAS (group accounts only)	French GAAP and IAS (in respect of consolidation rules) with US GAAP conversion permitted
Interim reporting	Bi-anually	Quarterly	Quarterly	Bi-annually, but turnover must be reported quarterly

* figures as at 31 December 2001

disclosure requirements on markets such as AiM. A number of issues remain unresolved, and the final shape of regulation remains unclear. The present proposals are unlikely to help smaller quoted companies.

7

Selection of advisers

Andrew Black (Pinsent Curtis Biddle)

INTRODUCTION

The flotation of a company requires carefully coordinated teamwork by the company and its professional advisers.

This chapter seeks to provide a description of the company's advisers and their respective roles. The more specific tasks and documents for which each adviser is normally directly responsible are set out in detail in the appendix at the end of the chapter.

As soon as a company has decided on a flotation, the directors' first step should be to identify and appoint the sponsor for the listing. The sponsor will coordinate the company's entry to the market. The board will also need a corporate broker, which may or may not be the same firm as that sponsoring the issue. Further advisers needed for the flotation include reporting accountants, solicitors and tax specialists (usually accountants or lawyers) and the directors will also probably decide to use both public and investor relations advisers.

SELECTION OF ADVISERS

Choosing good quality corporate advisers is one of the first and most important things that a company must do in preparation for a listing. It is also one of the most difficult.

The sheer range of different aspects on which the company needs advice means that it requires an equally wide range of professional advisers, each looking after their own specific area of specialization. Some areas of responsibility, such as the roles of sponsor and corporate broker, can potentially be combined by a single firm. Moves towards multi-disciplinary partnerships for professionals such as lawyers and accountants may also open the way for greater combination in those aspects. However, many directors feel it is actually in a company's best interests to have separate advisers for each area, since it may lessen the potential for conflicts of interests in the event of any problems or unforeseen developments.

The natural starting-point in the company's directors' search for suitable professional advisers to guide them through the listing process is to talk to the company's existing advisers, usually accountants and solicitors. The directors should start this process at least a year before they intend to join the market, although they may ultimately find that the process takes less time than they expected. The company's existing solicitors and accountants may already possess the necessary expertise, experience and resources to act for it on the flotation. If not, they will certainly be able to recommend and introduce the directors to suitable firms of advisers that can provide independent guidance.

Many companies approach the appointment of advisers by holding 'beauty parades' with a series of them, asking each about their expertise and fees, and getting a feeling for what it would be like to work closely with them over an extended period. The directors will be spending a considerable amount of time (and money) with their chosen advisers, and the relationship may well continue after the flotation, so it is crucial that they can get on with them on a personal level. The directors should also investigate the potential scope for negotiation on costs and areas of responsibilities.

81

ADVISERS' ROLES

The sponsor

The first concrete step towards flotation is to identify and appoint a suitable sponsor for the listing. The sponsor takes a central role in the flotation process, advising the company on a wide range of issues, probably including the appointment of other professional advisers. An investment bank, stockbroker or other adviser such as a corporate finance house or accountancy firm can take on the role of sponsor, provided they are approved by the London Stock Exchange to do so. A full list of approved sponsors can be obtained from the Exchange.

Since acting as a sponsor also requires a high degree of commitment from the firm taking on the role, the appointment process is essentially two-way. The board will certainly want to look at the potential sponsor's expertise, experience and likely fees. However, the sponsor will also want to have a good look at the company's business before agreeing to take on its flotation. It is a good idea to prepare in advance a summary briefing on the company's business and financial history for each prospective sponsor.

Although the precise valuation of the business will not be decided until the eve of the flotation, many better informed companies make a discussion about company valuation a part of the beauty parades for their sponsor. As a would-be issuer, it is also sensible for the directors to conduct research into the quoted companies in their own sector, to give them some idea of the methods of valuation and the kind of rating they might expect from the market. This will ensure that the management can have a meaningful discussion with the parading sponsors.

It is also advisable at this stage for management to question the sponsor about the likely investor base for the issue. If the sponsor is well prepared, it should be able to discuss the proportion of the issue that should go to investors specializing in the company's sector or perhaps to funds with an international flavour, and will have the evidence to back up its opinions. Much of this advice can apply to the appointment of the broker as well.

If the board and the potential sponsor are still interested in one another after the initial meeting, the sponsor will then require more detailed financial information, and will probably want to come and look at the company's operations and premises before accepting the business. Essentially, the sponsor will want to be sure that the company's business and its management are appropriate for a listing, and that the flotation stands a very good chance of success. So, as well as assessing the sponsor's abilities and fees, it is the directors' job to convince them of their own company's strength and prospects.

The sponsor's pivotal role, and its responsibilities both to the company and to the Exchange, means it has to undertake a wide range of duties all the way through the flotation process. Many of these duties will overlap with the company's own assessment of its suitability, in areas such as management depth and financial controls. First of all, the sponsor will assess the company's general suitability for a listing, in the light of its organizational structure and capital requirements. It will then advise on the structure and make-up of the board, the best method of flotation for the company, and the flotation timetable. It will also assist (if required) with the appointment of other advisers, and coordinate their activities once they are on the team. As the flotation approaches, the sponsor will advise on the pricing and underwriting of the shares, and the relevant marketing strategy for the issue.

In an AiM flotation the role of the nominated adviser or 'nomad' is very similar to that of a sponsor to a full listing. The nomad is responsible for confirming to the Stock Exchange that the applicant is suitable for admission and the AiM rules (on admission and continuing obligations) are complied with. Like the sponsor to a full listing, the nomad will coordinate the entire application process and, following admission, will continue to provide advice and guidance generally as the company's financial adviser.

The main differences between the obligations of sponsors under the Listing Rules and those of nominated advisers are as follows. First, while nominated advisers and sponsors are required to confirm that the relevant requirements have been met, the sponsors are in addition required to satisfy themselves, having made due and careful enquiry, that all relevant matters regarding suitability for admission have been drawn to the Exchange's attention. Secondly, certain specific duties of sponsors under the Listing Rules (for example confirmation in respect of financial reporting procedures, the report on the working capital statement and report on profit forecast) do not apply to nominated advisers.

The corporate broker

The corporate broker acts as the board's main interface with the stock market and potential investors. The firm of brokers appointed will assess the current conditions in the stock market, and provide vital feedback on investors' likely response to the issue. If the appointed sponsor is an integrated firm offering both investment banking and stockbroking services, then the directors may decide that they also want them to take on the role of corporate broker. Again, the sponsor will help and advise on the selection of the right firm, although it may be advisable to see a number of them to compare their fees and approach. A useful guide is to look at the other companies that the prospective broker has acted for, which will give the board some idea of its standing and areas of expertise. For example, if the company is in the high-tech sphere, it may want a broker that has a solid track record in stimulating investor interest in technology businesses. The board may also want to be sure that its chosen broker appears in the league tables of leading research houses for the company's particular sector.

As well as advising the board and its sponsor on market conditions and the likely level of demand, the corporate broker also actively markets the shares to potential investors, and can advise on the best method, size, timing and price. It can put in place market-related arrangements such as sub-underwriting and placing agreements. It will also help the company meet the Exchange's listing requirements, and usually continues to work with the company after the flotation to maintain its shares' liquidity and profile in the aftermarket.

Similarly, in an AiM flotation, the nominated broker or 'nobo' will provide a point of contact with the investment community, will help in fundraising and will be responsible for creating and maintaining a market in the company's shares. Thus the broker will use his or her best endeavours to find matching business if there is no market maker registered in the security and will also provide information to the market through the Stock Exchange Alternative Trading Service, SEATS Plus, on which AiM securities are traded. The nominated broker is also required to input to SEATS Plus useful information on the company such as the number of shares in issue, percentage of shares in public hands, turnover, profit after tax, dates of announcement of annual and interim results and dividends.

The reporting accountant

The role of reporting accountant in a flotation is separate from that of the company's existing auditors, but can be (and often is) fulfilled by a separate team in the same firm if the directors so choose. The sponsors may want to appoint a different firm to ensure the highest possible level of detachment and independence in this key role. Essentially, the reporting accountant is responsible for reviewing the company's financial record for potential investors, and thus has an influence on their decision as to whether to buy the shares.

As the company goes through the flotation process, the directors will hear a lot about 'long form' and 'short form' reports. The difference is quite simple. The 'long form' report, as the name suggests, is a detailed financial and management history of the business. It is not published, but does provide the management and sponsors with the information needed to draft the prospectus. It also serves as the basis for the reporting accountants' 'short form' report, which is published as part of the prospectus itself. The reporting accountants will also usually prepare a report for the sponsor on the company's projected working capital position over the 12 to 18 months following flotation. They may also advise on the tax implications of the flotation, or the board may have decided to appoint separate tax specialists to do this.

Lawyers

Most flotations involve two separate sets of lawyers – one to advise the company and its existing shareholders, and the other to advise the sponsor. The responsibilities of the company's lawyers, with whom the directors will of course have the most contact, include overseeing the changes to the company's articles of association and directors' contracts, and possibly re-registering the company as a plc. They also prepare the painstaking 'verification' questions, which are used to confirm that every single statement in the prospectus can be justified as fact. The rigours of this process mean that management will get to know their lawyers very well. The company's lawyers will also work alongside the sponsor's lawyers on the necessary agreements between the company, the sponsor and the existing shareholders, covering aspects like underwriting and tax. The board might also want them to draw up share option schemes for staff, to be introduced with the flotation.

Other advisers

Depending on the method of the flotation and the specific circumstances of the company, the directors might also decide to use a number of other advisers in particular areas. The most likely is a firm of financial public relations consultants to maximize the degree of positive awareness of the company and its products or services, among both the general public and the professional investment community in the run-up to the flotation. Companies coming to market often underestimate the importance of public profile and press contacts. The company's financial PR advisers should also help ensure that any public statements and press releases are permissible under the relevant disclosure regulations. The board will also find that by helping to generate ongoing press interest and publicity, its financial PR advisers can play a key role in sustaining awareness and liquidity after the listing. The management might consider media training for those key directors who will be under the spotlight.

The company may also require a number of other advisers. These include registrars to manage the company's share register; chartered surveyors or valuers to assess property values; security printers for safe, accurate and speedy production of documentation; actuaries to assess the position of company pension schemes; receiving bankers to handle share applications (only in a public offer); and insurance brokers to check that all risks are adequately covered.

APPENDIX: LIST OF DOCUMENTS FOR A FLOTATION

Set out below is a typical list of documents required for an offer, indicating the professional adviser primarily responsible.

Sponsor

Pathfinder prospectus
Prospectus
Mini prospectus
Administration – timetable, list of parties and documents
Application form/preferential application form
Newspaper advertisement(s)
Abridged advertisements/formal notices
Model Code for directors' share dealings
Letter for publication on profit forecast (if applicable)
Sponsor's required declaration/confirmations to the Stock Exchange
Letter to the Stock Exchange on working capital
Capital reorganization
Press announcements
Consent letter
Expenses estimate

Stockbroker

Marketing logistics
Research material
Presentation material for investor presentations
Directors' declaration cards
Application for listing

Particulars of securities being listed
Declaration as to filing of documents
Sub-underwriting/placing letters
Letter of derogation and non-applicability
Letter of comfort in respect of sponsor's declaration

Solicitors to the company and to the issue

Memorandum and Articles of Association
Capital reorganization
Company resolutions
Letters of allotment
Re-registration as a public limited company (if applicable)
Memorandum on directors' responsibilities
Directors' responsibility statements
Powers of attorney
Underwriting agreement (including warranties and indemnity)
Profit sharing and other employee share schemes (if applicable)
Share option scheme (if applicable)
Directors' service agreements
Material contracts and litigation review
Certificates of incorporation and re-registration
Certificates of titles to properties
Verification notes
Completion agenda
Board minutes for completion meeting
Documents for display
Letter of comfort in respect of sponsor's declaration

Reporting accountants

Long form report
Short form report (if applicable)
Statement of adjustments (if applicable)
Indebtedness statement
Confirmation of bank facilities
Memorandum on working capital

Memorandum on profit forecast (if applicable)
Letter for publication on profit forecast (if applicable)
Consent letter (if applicable)
Tax clearances
Comfort letter on financial information, controls and procedures and other matters (such as future taxation)
Letter of advice on tax indemnities, and close company status
Letter of comfort in respect of sponsor's declaration

Public relations consultants

Presentation material for press and analyst presentations
Statutory and corporate advertising
Artwork for prospectus/covers
Press announcements

Receiving bankers and registrars

Receiving bankers' agreement
Letter of acceptance
Share registration
Regret letter

Other

Pension scheme valuation (if applicable)
Property valuation (if applicable)
Market, environmental and other specialist reports (as applicable)

8

The role of the sponsor

Colin Aaronson (Grant Thornton)

SUMMARY

- The company's adviser in a flotation is either a sponsor (Full List) or a nominated adviser (AiM).
- Their official role is regulatory – the fundraising will be managed by the broker.
- In practical terms, their job is to project manage the flotation.

INTRODUCTION

The first person to contact for anyone thinking about floating their company will be a financial adviser. For a flotation on the Full List that adviser will be a sponsor, and for AiM a nominated adviser or nomad. If the company, or its auditors or solicitors, does not have any suitable contacts, a list of sponsors is kept by the UKLA, and the London Stock Exchange maintains a register of nomads.

There are two main differences between the two roles. First, an AiM company must have a nomad at all times. It cannot be admitted without one, and if a nomad resigns, trading in the company's securities will be suspended until it has appointed a new nomad (and the company will have its admission cancelled if it fails to appoint one within a month of suspension). A Full List company only needs to appoint a sponsor when it is either applying for listing or preparing a circular in respect of a large transaction, or when the UKLA instructs it to appoint one to deal with a breach of the Listing Rules. These rules reflect the fact that AiM companies are smaller and arguably in greater need of guidance than those on the List.

Secondly, a nomad must decide if a company is suitable for admission to AiM. The Exchange has powers to delay admission, or make it subject to special conditions, but the responsibility for deciding on suitability belongs to the nomad. By contrast, a sponsor need only satisfy itself that its client has complied with the Listing Rules – it is the UKLA and the London Stock Exchange that determine the suitability of companies seeking admission to the Full List.

Both sponsor and nomad will project manage the flotation. During the flotation process, a sponsor will liaise with the UKLA, submitting drafts of the Listing Particulars for approval. Only once the UKLA has approved or 'stamped' the document can a company join the Full List.

By contrast, it is up to the nomad to approve the AiM admission document, and it will only do so once it has satisfied itself that it contains all the information required by the AiM Rules, and that it contains sufficient information to allow investors to make an informed decision whether to invest.

For simplicity, we will refer to both types of adviser as a nomad, and both types of admission document as a prospectus when discussing the flotation process.

What type of nomad?

The company must start by appointing the nomad. This is the company's financial adviser, privy to confidential information, and the arbiter of what information is appropriate to be put in the public domain. Before flotation, such information will be included in the prospectus; after flotation it will be released via a regulatory news service. This advisory function is generally described as 'corporate finance'. On the other hand the sales side of the broker, whose primary function is to raise funds, may be regarded as a member of the public from the point of view of information released to it.

A nomad may be the same firm as the broker. In these 'integrated houses', a Chinese Wall separates the corporate finance (nomad) and the broking function. However, the nomad and the broker may be different firms. In this situation, there is a clear separation of the two functions, although a member of the broking firm's corporate finance department is usually part of the team advising on the flotation, and is the point of contact with the brokers. Larger firms of brokers tend to perform both roles, whereas smaller brokers are less likely to have a corporate finance department authorized to act as a nomad.

There are advantages to having an independent nomad, as well as to having both roles performed by the same firm. The principal benefit cited for using an integrated house is cost saving. The principal benefit cited for using an independent nomad is the genuinely independent advice such a firm offers in selecting and negotiating terms with the broker. In practice, the company is likely to base its decision on personal contacts and recommendations, or simply to appoint whoever agrees to raise the money.

Whichever type of nomad is appointed, that firm will start the flotation process.

THE FLOTATION PROCESS

Appointment of advisers

Before the flotation process can begin, certain advisers need to be appointed in addition to the nomad. The key advisers in a flotation are shown in Table 8.1.

The nomad, broker, reporting accountant and solicitors to the company are all crucial, and the flotation process cannot begin until

Table 8.1 *Key advisers in a flotation*

Title	Function
Nomad	Dealing with regulatory aspects of admission, project management
Broker	Raising funds, usually by a placing of shares with institutional, and occasionally private clients
Solicitors to the company	Detailed legal input into, and verification of prospectus. Conducting legal due diligence and dealing with legal matters relating to the company's status, share issues, contracts, etc
Reporting accountant	Reviewing and reporting on working capital forecasts, and financial control procedures, producing accounting information required for prospectus. Conducting due diligence on the company and report to nomad
Solicitor to the placing	Preparing placing agreement between company and its broker
Registrar	Registration and transfer of shares. Usually deals with application to have shares traded in dematerialized form via CREST
Financial public relations firm	Assisting the company in promoting the issue to potential investors. Raising the profile and increasing awareness of the company

they have been appointed. The other professionals can be appointed at a later date.

The company will engage each of these professionals directly, with the exception of the solicitors to the placing, who are appointed by the brokers. However, the company will bear all the costs, which are generally paid out of the placing proceeds.

Starting the flotation process

Once the company and its advisers have agreed to proceed with a flotation, and the key professionals have been appointed and their terms of engagement agreed, the nomad will call on all parties to attend a meeting to agree a timetable and clearly identify responsibilities. This timetable must be adhered to if the process is not to drift. The nomad will also circulate a detailed list of parties with contact details, and a list of documents to be produced.

The nomad will take as its starting point the end of the flotation process. The key date is known as 'Impact Day', and it is on this day that the prospectus is finalized and registered at Companies House, and posted to potential investors. Admission to the Full List or AiM, and receipt of funds, usually takes place shortly thereafter.

The company will usually need or want to secure funds by a particular date, and this will determine Impact Day. The broker will advise when would be a good time to introduce the company to the market, having regard to Christmas, Easter and summer holidays, market sentiment, and their own workload. From this point, the nomad will work backwards setting dates for the completion of the final prospectus, the placing proof and the pathfinder if applicable, completion of the various accountants' and experts' reports, and legal and commercial due diligence.

Central to the nomad's work, and indeed that of all the professional advisers, is the preparation of the prospectus. The considerable amount of work that the professional advisers undertake revolves around preparing a document that describes accurately and in sufficient detail the business and activities, financial information and legal structure of the company.

The prospectus

All prospectuses have a common structure, even if the size, style and contents differ considerably. The four parts of a prospectus, each of which can comprise a number of sections, are as follows.

1. The very front
This includes a cover page, whose contents are determined by the AiM Rules, the Pos Regs, or the Listing Rules, as appropriate. The next few pages contain an index, a list of directors and advisers, glossaries and lists of definitions, placing or offer statistics, and an

expected timetable of principal events. The contents of this section will flow from what is contained in the rest of the document.

2. The front end

The front end contains what is, in effect, the investment proposition. It is also the basis on which the company is being admitted to either AiM or the Full List. The front end usually contains the following information:

- history of the business;
- information about the present day business of the company;
- summarized information about key personnel;
- information about the placing or offer for subscription;
- the company's policy on corporate governance;
- share option arrangements and dividend policy;
- risk factors.

3. The accounting information

The information contained in this section usually goes in the middle of the document. It is determined by the Pos Regs or the Listing Rules, and comprises the following:

- summarized audited accounts for three complete years prior to flotation, and sometimes interim accounts to a later date;
- the reporting accountants' opinion as to whether the financial information shows a true and fair view for the purposes of the prospectus;
- certain statutory information.

There may be accounting information required for more than one company, if the prospectus relates to the acquisition of one company by another, and the flotation of the enlarged group.

4. The back end

This section contains what is known as the statutory and general information. Its contents are determined by the Pos Regs or Listing Rules, and contains details of the following:

95

- responsibility statements (directors must accept responsibility for every statement contained in the prospectus);
- details of the incorporation and legal status of the company, its registered office, and its objects;
- information about share capital, including authorities to issue further shares;
- summarized information about the company's Memorandum and Articles of Association, dealing particularly with voting rights, transfer of shares, dividends and borrowing powers. It will also deal with the appointment, responsibilities, powers and procedure for determining the remuneration of directors;
- directors' interests in the company and directorships with other companies;
- substantial shareholders;
- share option plans;
- material contracts;
- summarized tax position;
- the working capital adequacy statement;
- sundry other information.

It may be necessary or considered desirable to reproduce experts' reports. These are usually inserted before the back end or before the accounting information.

Setting the scope

The nomad will need to set the scope of three pieces of work that the reporting accountants will undertake:

1. A 'long form' report, which is a report on the operations and activities of the company. It is a private document that is usually addressed to the nomad, broker and the company itself. It is not published. The nomad will set the scope of the due diligence that forms the basis for this report, based on its knowledge of the business and its assessment of areas of risk. Brokers can provide valuable input into the process, being able to draw on the knowledge of their analysts.

2. A 'short form' report, which contains the accounting information that is required for the prospectus. The reporting accountants should understand the requirements, but the responsibility for deciding what information goes into the report belongs to the nomad.
3. The working capital report. The minimum period is 12 months, but it is up to the nomad to decide what period the reporting accountants should report on.

The nomad will also become involved in determining the areas that the solicitors will cover as part of their legal due diligence. A lot of the work will be based on verification of documents referred to in the prospectus, but the nomad may ask the solicitors to investigate areas of concern or vulnerability. Where a company is dependent on intellectual property, this may form the subject of a specific review.

For the Full List, 'competent persons' (as defined in the Listing Rules) are instructed to report on mineral companies and experts are required to report on scientific research based companies as well as on innovative high growth companies whose products or services are unproven. For other types of company seeking admission to the Full List and for AiM companies, even if an expert's report is not required by the rules, a report on the company's markets or technology may be considered desirable, particularly for high technology businesses. With these types of report, again it is the nomad who sets the scope of the work.

Starting work

The order in which work starts will depend on what information is available. Typically, the first task would fall on the reporting accountants who would begin work on the long form report. While their work is underway the lawyers would commence drafting the statutory and general information section of the prospectus. The nomad and the company would begin work on the front part of the prospectus and the reporting accountants would draft the short form report for inclusion in the prospectus.

If any commercial due diligence has to be undertaken or any expert's reports prepared, this work will commence at a very early stage.

Meanwhile, the company would be required to prepare working capital forecasts in support of the statement as to the adequacy of working capital that the directors have to make in the prospectus. The forecasts should comprise a pack containing income statement, cash flow and balance sheet forecasts together with underlying assumptions. These forecasts will normally be required to cover a period of at least 18 months from the date of the prospectus.

On completion of the draft long form report, a full first draft of the prospectus will be drawn together under the supervision of the nomad. The reporting accountants would then typically begin work on their review of the working capital forecasts. During this part of the process, the prospectus will go through a number of drafts. As the content of the prospectus settles down, the lawyers will begin work on the verification process, and the brokers will begin to sound out the market informally as to who might be interested in taking the shares to be issued. The PR advisers would work on the press coverage to be sought for the issue.

If a pathfinder prospectus is to be produced, it is likely to be required some 10 to 14 days before Impact Day. This is an essentially complete document (save for agreement as to the price at which the shares are to be placed), which can be taken to potential institutional investors in order to gauge interest and determine the placing price. During this period the company is often required to make presentations to potential investors.

Occasionally, the company issues a 'placing proof', sometimes described as a 'P Proof'. This is in all material respects a finished document, except it is marked as a proof. The broker gives this document to potential investors to secure their commitment to invest prior to completing and registering the prospectus itself. A placing proof will be used if there is some doubt as to the success of the fundraising, or where the nomad and broker want to know the amount raised prior to finalizing the prospectus. Where changes occur between the placing proof and the final prospectus, the investors will be notified of these changes, and given the opportunity to reconsider their decision to invest.

Once the brokers are confident that the funds will be raised, and at what price, the company is ready to complete its prospectus, and a completion meeting will be arranged for the day before Impact Day. At this meeting, all documents will be signed and the directors will formally approve and take responsibility for the prospectus. Many other documents including the verification notes which record the underlying evidence for statements contained in the prospectus will be completed and signed, and the order given for bulk printing of the prospectus. This is then printed overnight, and on Impact Day it is filed with the relevant authorities and distributed to shareholders or potential investors, or in fact to anyone interested in receiving a copy.

With an institutional placing, admission usually takes place within a fortnight of Impact Day. The flotation process may continue for about a month after Impact Day, either if there is an 'Offer for Subscription' to the general public, or if the company's shareholders need to approve any aspect of the transaction in a general meeting.

A typical timetable

Each flotation is different, but the flotation process is likely to pan out in the way shown in Table 8.2.

The work of the nomad

Apart from project managing the flotation process and coordinating the work of the various parties, the nomad will need to liaise with the AiM team at the London Stock Exchange. An AiM company will need to issue a statement of its intention to seek admission to AiM 10 working days before the proposed date of admission. The nomad will draft and issue that statement. It will also arrange the formal application, which must arrive at least three working days before admission.

Table 8.2 *Countdown to an AIM listing*

	Company	Nomad/ Sponsor	Reporting Accountant	Broker	Lawyer	PR
12–24 weeks before admission						
Appoint advisers	✓	✓				
Give detailed instructions to all advisers	✓	✓	✓	✓	✓	✓
Detailed timetable agreed	✓	✓	✓	✓	✓	✓
Board appointments	✓					
6–12 weeks before admission						
Corporate structure	✓	✓				
Commence reporting accountant work*	✓	✓	✓			
Review of problem areas (ongoing)	✓	✓	✓		✓	
Draft prospectus produced		✓		✓		
Initial review of pricing issues		✓	✓			
First drafting meetings	✓	✓		✓	✓	
Commence legal due diligence	✓	✓		✓	✓	
Review PR presentations						✓
Analyst presentation	✓	✓				✓
1–6 weeks before admission						
Complete reporting accountant work and legal due diligence	✓	✓	✓		✓	
Drafting meetings	✓	✓	✓		✓	
Due diligence on prospectus	✓	✓	✓	✓	✓	
PR meetings and roadshow	✓				✓	
Verification						
Week of admission						
All documents completed and approved	✓	✓	✓	✓	✓	
Pricing and allocation	✓	✓		✓		
Register prospectus		✓			✓	

*Commence with work on long form report and short form report, followed by working capital and other letters
Source: Grant Thornton

As far as the process of producing a document is concerned, the main difference between an AiM admission document and Listing Particulars is that the UKLA has to approve the document, and does so through a process of pre-vetting. The UKLA will see successive drafts of the Listing Particulars and comment on them in detail. This process is complete once the UKLA has approved or 'stamped' the document. The sponsor will handle the formal application to the London Stock Exchange.

Where a flotation involves a smaller public company acquiring a larger one (a reverse takeover) and the flotation of the enlarged group, the nomad will have to deal with the Takeover Panel to ensure that the document complies with the relevant provisions of the City Code. This can involve lengthy discussions and negotiations with the Takeover Panel.

Once the prospectus is complete, the nomad will arrange for it to be distributed and will work with the financial PR agents to ensure the transaction is appropriately publicized.

FOLLOWING FLOTATION

A sponsor's duties formally end once the company is on the market. By contrast, the responsibilities of a nomad continue after admission, and until such time as it is replaced as nomad, or the company leaves the market.

A nomad's principal ongoing obligation is to advise its AiM company clients on their obligations under the AiM Rules. Much of the work will involve advising on the need for announcements, their form and content. Companies must tread a fine line between ensuring the market is adequately informed, and creating a misleading impression that the company is more dynamic than is actually the case. While in general more information is better than less, care has to be taken to ensure that the announcement is not misleading, for the consequences of misleading the market under the Financial Services and Markets Act 2000 can be severe. Although it is the company that is obliged to release announcements, and the nomad's responsibility is merely to advise its clients, in practice the nomad will often release the announcement to the market on its client's behalf.

Where the market is not aware of an important event or fact relating to the company, and the share price does not reflect that information, a 'disorderly market' in the shares is said to exist. The nomad will maintain close contact with its clients to ensure that the market is aware of information that needs to be in the public domain.

Companies will often ask their nomad for advice on certain issues that are not specifically covered in the AiM Rules, such as the suitability of share option arrangements or related party contracts. The brokers will advise on what investors will find acceptable; the nomad must advise on what is appropriate from the point of view of corporate governance and for the protection of the market's reputation.

When a company enters into a transaction that might need to be disclosed under the AiM Rules, the nomad will advise the company on its position and may need to clarify certain issues and even negotiate with the AiM team.

However, the nomad's ultimate responsibility is to judge the suitability of a company for admission to, and continued listing on AiM. That responsibility starts from when the nomad is asked to act for the company and continues throughout the flotation process and for as long as the company is on the market. If the nomad believes that its client is no longer suitable for admission, it must resign its position. This is not an easy decision, as there are shareholders whose interests may be at stake. Nevertheless, the nomad's primary duty of care is owed to the London Stock Exchange, and it is the Exchange's interests which are paramount.

9

The role of the lawyers

Hannah Kendrick (Pinsent Curtis Biddle)

INTRODUCTION – GENERAL ROLE

The role of the lawyer in the flotation process will cover many different areas, including the preparation and review of documentation and general advice on complicated areas of law. The principal responsibility of the lawyer is to prepare the necessary documentation, to ensure compliance with the applicable law and regulations and to assist (specifically on the legal aspects but not exclusively so) on the project management of the transaction. The work of the lawyer will be essential in meeting the target timetable for the project and ensuring the smooth running of the process.

Though obviously not able to advise in detail on the commercial advantages and disadvantages of each of the principal stock exchanges available to a company for fundraising, the lawyer can be a sounding board to determine the merits, compliance requirements, documentation and other issues that apply to each market and to highlight the differences between a full listing, listing on AiM, OFEX or any of the other recognized exchanges – and even to give a view on other international exchanges (eg Paris, New York or Japan). Often, the identification of the correct market is determined on the balance of the legal and financial requirements to be met against the level of funding required. An experienced adviser may also assist on whether an offer of shares to the public is the appropriate route for the company or whether other sources of funds, such as venture capital, should be considered. A comparison of the regulatory frameworks relating to flotations is made in Chapter 5.

The general role of the lawyers in a flotation will be to provide advice on a number of issues including:

- the advantages and disadvantages of obtaining a listing from the point of view of legal requirements;
- the choice of appropriate stock exchange;
- the suitability of the constitution of the company for flotation and the compliance of the company with listing requirements;
- the flotation procedure and timing;
- the preparation, publication and verification of listing particulars;
- the compliance of the officers of the company to their ongoing responsibilities; and
- the legal consequences of going public and the legal restrictions on the businesses which arise.

In Chapter 7 the process of selecting your legal adviser was discussed. There are a large number of factors involved in determining this, but in the main it is a balance of two factors, which are not necessarily mutually exclusive, being first the need to select and instruct an experienced and competent legal adviser who is capable of carrying out the wider range of complex legal work required, and secondly ensuring that the legal adviser provides a value-for-money service.

THE PARTICULAR ROLE OF THE LEGAL ADVISERS

Corporate lawyers are principally retained to guide companies effectively through the particular legal aspects of the fundraising process.

However, a client may rely on his or her corporate lawyers for advice on a range of commercial issues, not necessarily relating to purely legal aspects of the process. Although a few lawyers would be reluctant to formally advise on any matter other than legal issues, those corporate lawyers who have considerable experience in dealing with flotations and other public issues of securities are often able from experience to give straightforward common sense assistance to clients who are encountering certain problems for the first time.

In particular, the legal adviser can provide advice and guidance on the initial steps to flotation and the basic conditions for listing set out below:

- Are the securities eligible for listing?
- Has a sponsor been appointed?
- Have the requirements of the listing authority in respect of company accounts been satisfied?
- Has the necessary trading record for the appropriate market been satisfied?
- Is the company in compliance with its governing legislation and is its business undertaken in accordance with the constitutional documents by which it is regulated?
- Do the company's constitutional documents comply with the provisions of listing legislation?
- Is sufficient share capital of the company available for distribution to the public to meet the requirements of the relevant stock exchange?
- Is senior management able to demonstrate responsibility for the company's major businesses throughout the period of its required trading record?
- Is there a controlling shareholder? If yes, has an agreement been entered into regulating its position if this is required under the appropriate listing regulation?

In working through the above questions with senior management and the other advisers, the legal adviser will assist the company to reach the major decisions about its business and the proposed flotation.

Legal advisers to whom?

A typical flotation will involve:

- a company whose securities are to be listed and which may be raising capital by the issue of new shares;
- shareholders of the company who may be selling shares in the flotation to realize all or part of their investment;
- a merchant bank, which may underwrite the share offer and act as sponsor (these roles are sometimes assumed by a broker alone where a merchant bank is not involved);
- a broker who is responsible for the marketing of the offering, either with a view to identifying those who wish definitely to acquire securities as placees and/or those who are prepared to sub-underwrite the offering;
- investors who may be institutional or private clients of the broker or members of the general public;
- the relevant stock exchange.

It is possible that lawyers are advising the first four of those parties identified above in respect of the flotation.

Nevertheless, there are two sets of legal advisers who play the dominant role in a flotation. The company's solicitors will normally be responsible for the preparation of legal documentation in relation to the issue, for advising the directors of their responsibilities both in relation to the prospectus and following the flotation, for conducting a review of the company's existing contractual and other legal relations with third parties, and for advising the company in relation to any agreement entered into with the nominated adviser. They will also deal with the verification of the whole of the prospectus as well as producing the information section or so-called 'back end' of the prospectus.

A different firm will act as solicitors to the issue, primarily to advise the broker/merchant bank in relation to matters where the company's solicitors would have a conflict of interest, such as any placing agreement relating to the broker/merchant bank's obligation to identify new shareholders for the company.

The solicitors to the issue are also responsible for ensuring that all legal requirements associated with the issue are met and that verification of the prospectus with the assistance of the company's solicitors is thoroughly undertaken.

Specific role of lawyers to the company

Concentrating in particular on the company's lawyers, their specific role will require them to:

- ensure compliance with the regulatory framework appropriate to the market on which the shares will be listed;
- examine the company's Memorandum and Articles of Association to see if they are appropriate for the transition of the company to a quoted company. For example, any anachronistic voting structures or restrictions will need to be removed;
- assist the company in creating the group structure appropriate for a listing;
- assist the company in re-registering as a public company in accordance with sections 42–47 of the Companies Act 1985;
- support the company and the financial adviser in structuring the offer and to document this structure;
- work with the company on verification of the offering document, ensuring that (wherever possible) statements are justified by reference to objective sources;
- assist in the production of the flotation documentation preparing, where appropriate, wording to comply with listing requirements;
- advise on the ongoing compliance requirements under the rules of the relevant stock exchange and under the general law.

The company may consider setting up an employee share scheme if it has not already done so. The purpose of this would be to incentivize employees at a time when their commitment to the company is crucial. The company's lawyers will generally advise the company in the setting up of any such scheme.

Although the role of overall project manager of the flotation should normally be that of the sponsor, the legal adviser will project manage the legal aspects of the transaction and will assist in the overall project management process.

DUE DILIGENCE

A flotation cannot progress without due diligence being undertaken. The legal due diligence process revolves around a detailed questionnaire prepared by the legal advisers to the company and revised by the legal advisers to the sponsor, the answers to which form the basis of the legal due diligence report, again prepared by the company's legal advisers and reviewed by those of the sponsor. There will be a great deal of time spent in putting together and reviewing the information for this report, both verbal and written. Depending on the nature of the company's business the main headings to be covered will include title to the company's properties, environmental issues, litigation, intellectual property ownership and licences, pension schemes, banking arrangements, material contracts, employment terms, constitutional documents, share capital, competition and trade regulations, licences and insurance. The report will highlight the areas that are made known to the general public in the offer document under existing legislation and also any particular areas of concern to which reference should be made.

As well as gathering together the information required for the prospectus, the company's legal advisers should be checking that the company has proper title to the key assets of the business. They will also be looking out for any unusual obligations or liabilities that might affect the company's value. For example, any unresolved litigation, for which no provision has been made in the accounts, should be highlighted, as should any unduly heavy reliance on a particular supplier or customer.

The second form of due diligence is the verification process. The company's solicitors will prepare a detailed series of questions seeking objective evidence of the correctness of each statement made in the offer document. The directors will then take responsibility for those statements through their answers to these questions and produce, where possible, independent evidence of the factual basis for those statements. Through this process, directors can obtain comfort that each statement made by them in the offer document can be independently verified. The questions and answers are reviewed by the legal advisers to the sponsor to ensure that evidence is provided wherever practicable.

DOCUMENTATION

There are a large number of documents to be drafted, negotiated and finally settled for flotation. The principal documentation to be provided will include:

- The offer document – the precise nature of this will vary depending on the nature of the offer and whether it is to be underwritten by any sponsor or broker. Its principal terms will be to ensure that the sponsor or broker obtain shareholders for the new shares to be issued or transferred (or possibly to take up the shares itself if it fails to do so). The offer document will also contain warranties and indemnities from the directors of the company to the sponsor or broker on their own behalf and on behalf of the shareholders they identify, together with restrictions on future sales of shares by directors and by major shareholders.
- An application form under which prospective shareholders may undertake to take up the shares, or a placing letter under which the sponsor or broker will place shares with prospective new shareholders.
- A raft of additional supporting documentation to effect the flotation in compliance with the rules of the relevant exchange, including directors' declarations, powers of attorney, directors' responsibility letters, appointment letters for agents/bankers/ merchant bankers, verification notes and board minutes.

The above list is not exhaustive and depends on the nature of the flotation.

In particular, the company's lawyer will advise and negotiate on its behalf the offering agreement with the issuing house, especially the warranties and indemnities sought by the sponsor from the directors and/or principal shareholders.

The sanctions for negligently or dishonestly raising finance through the issue of shares are great and, therefore, extreme care must be taken in preparing all of the above documentation.

CONTINUING OBLIGATIONS

Following flotation, the company and its directors will be subject to continuing obligations on which its lawyers will advise. These include:

- the requirements of the listing rules of the relevant stock exchange on general and specific disclosure obligations, the content and timing of release of circulars, press announcements and other information concerning the company;
- the requirements of the Model Code on Directors' Dealings, if a listing is in the UK on the Full List or AiM;
- the preparation of annual reports and accounts in compliance with the relevant listing rules and statutes.

A more detailed discussion on these continuing obligations is provided in Chapter 16.

10

The role of the reporting accountant

Naomi Sharma (Grant Thornton)

SUMMARY

- A reporting accountant is required for any flotation.
- The reporting accountant reports on a number of areas, focusing on financial information, both historic and forecast.
- The reporting accountant is a valuable source of advice on various aspects of the flotation process, such as disclosure of information or improvements to company procedures.

INTRODUCTION

The reporting accountant (RA) is a key member of the team of advisers for a flotation and takes responsibility for reviewing and reporting on a number of areas, including historic and forecast financial information. The RA's financial expertise and experience with companies going public will help smooth the flotation process as the RA can quickly identify and resolve issues that might otherwise hold up the process.

The RA also brings a valuable independent perspective to the flotation process as the RA does not have a vested interest in its outcome. This independence enables the RA to express impartial views, even if these may seem unpopular at the time!

The company's directors have onerous responsibilities in relation to the investment circular[1] and the RA helps the directors discharge their responsibilities in a number of areas. Indeed the RA's work is a critical part of the process of 'due and careful enquiry' that underpins the investment circular.

This chapter examines the role of the RA in terms of the following areas:

- information in the investment circular;
- 'due diligence' reports on the company;
- other documents;
- other areas.

The RA's role is generally similar for flotations on AiM and the Official List; any differences are explained in the text.

INFORMATION IN THE INVESTMENT CIRCULAR

The RA has a number of areas of responsibility in relation to information disclosed in the investment circular, which are as follows:

- historic financial information;
- pro forma financial information;
- forecast financial information;
- other information.

Historic financial information

Potential investors need to understand the historic performance of the group[2] so that they can assess the extent to which this, together with other information in the investment circular, supports the proposed share price on flotation. The POS Regulations (AiM) and the Listing Rules (Official List) both require disclosure of historic information in the investment circular and the RA has an important role to play both in reporting on information and advising on how to deal with difficult areas.

Summary of requirements

Companies going public are usually required to disclose historic financial information for the three financial years prior to flotation, with some exceptions. If a company has not been trading for three years it can be admitted to AiM on the basis of a shorter period than three years. However, requirements for the Official List are stricter and a shorter period is only permitted if the UK Listing Authority agrees and the company meets the specific criteria of Chapter 25 of the Listing Rules (which imposes onerous requirements following flotation).

AiM and Official List have different requirements in relation to how 'old' the latest period (year) of financial information can be at flotation: the POS Regulations – latest period must be no more than nine months old; and Listing Rules – latest period must be no more than six months old.

The POS Regulations permit the inclusion of unaudited information if the latest period is out of date but the Listing Rules require such information to be audited.

The requirements in relation to financial information can be complex, for example, if there have been changes in group structure during the period, incorporation of a new holding company and so on. The RA can draw on considerable experience to help directors identify solutions to difficult areas.

Accountants' report (also called a short form report)
Historic financial information in the investment circular is usually included in a document called an accountants' report. This sets out the information in a similar format to the annual financial statements, except that there are three years of figures (unless the company has not been trading that long) and no directors' report is included. An accountants' report will comprise:

- the true and fair opinion of the RA (similar format to an audit report);
- accounting policies;
- profit and loss account;
- balance sheet;
- cash flow;
- notes.

If the company has subsidiaries, information will be presented on a consolidated basis for the group.

The RA takes responsibility for the information in the accountants' report and will need to perform sufficient procedures to be able to give a true and fair opinion on the information. The RA will normally review auditors' working papers (even if the same firm is RA and auditor) and determine whether any additional procedures need to be performed, for example, if the audit work appears insufficient or access is not permitted to working papers. In extreme cases this may involve re-performing audit work.

Sometimes companies going public have not been subject to audit, in which case the RA will need to perform a full audit on the historic financial information. This can be tricky in relation to the earlier years as supporting documentation may not be readily available. If a company that has not been subject to audit is contemplating going public then it is worthwhile having an audit, even if this is not a legal requirement, to reduce delays once the flotation process starts. Ensuring that historic financial information is of appropriate quality and is sufficiently up to date for inclusion in an investment circular is a key part of pre-flotation 'grooming' that will save considerable time and anguish in the flotation process.

In addition to providing a report on the historic financial information, the RA will often need to advise and assist in the presentation of the information in the accountants' report. Common areas that cause problems are:

- groups that have not been required to produce consolidated accounts;
- audited financial statements that do not have sufficient disclosures for the purposes of the investment circular – this is a particular issue for the Official List where the UKLA normally insists on the same level of disclosure as for a fully listed company, which is far more than many companies have experienced prior to flotation;
- financial statements with qualified opinions, as it is usually unacceptable for an accountants' report to contain a qualified opinion;
- changes in group structure during the three-year period.

The RA will advise on how to deal with such situations based on his or her previous knowledge and will discuss as necessary particular issues with the nomad or sponsor and, for the Official List, the UKLA.

Comparative table

For companies floating on the Official List, it is possible to include the historic financial information in a comparative table rather than an accountants' report. The key difference is that the comparative table does not include an opinion from the RA. There are strict criteria in the UK Listing Rules that must be met in order for this to be allowed.

Most sponsors will insist on an accountants' report for a company going public and comparative tables are usually only used when a quoted company seeks shareholder approval for a transaction (see Chapter 22 for information on transactions by quoted companies).

Pro forma financial information

The investment circular may include pro forma financial information to illustrate how the flotation affects the financial information of the company. The most common financial information is a pro forma statement of net assets that shows how the flotation proceeds will be initially allocated, for example in repayment of debt. The RA will often compile the pro forma financial information on the company's behalf and agree appropriate adjustments with the directors.

If such information is included the RA will provide a report that gives limited comfort on it. This report is similar in format to an audit report and includes an opinion along the following lines:

In our opinion:

- the pro forma financial information has been properly compiled on the basis stated;
- such basis is consistent with the accounting policies of the issuer;
- the adjustments are appropriate for the purposes of the pro forma financial information as disclosed [pursuant to paragraph 12.29 of the Listing Rules].

Forecast financial information

Disclosure of forecast financial information is relatively uncommon as it gives investors an obvious target to attack if the company does not meet expectations. However, in certain circumstances the nomad/sponsor may advise the company to include such information.

If forecast information is included the RA will provide a report that gives limited comfort on it. This report is similar in format to an audit report and includes an opinion along the following lines:

In our opinion the profit forecast, so far as the accounting policies and calculations are concerned, has been properly compiled on the bases and the assumptions stated by the directors of the company set out in Part X of the investment circular and has been prepared on a basis consistent with the accounting policies normally adopted by the group.

The RA's report is usually included in the investment circular.

The RA will have to perform specific procedures in order to give his or her report, such as testing the compilation of the forecast information. This work may be combined with the review for the working capital report that is discussed later in this section.

In relation to AiM only, the nomad is required to confirm that the forecast has been made after due and careful enquiry. The nomad may request the RA to provide comfort that this is the case in a private report addressed to the nomad. The exact nature of such a report would be agreed between the nomad and the RA.

'DUE DILIGENCE' REPORTS ON THE COMPANY

A substantial amount of the RA's time on a flotation will be spent on conducting due diligence on the company on behalf of its directors and the nomad or sponsor. This differs slightly to the due diligence process in relation to an acquisition or an application for funding, as two reports are produced and there are some additional requirements that are specific to a flotation. The two reports are known as a long form report and a working capital report.

Long form report

The long form report is a detailed report on every aspect of the company's business excluding forecasts, which are covered in the working capital report. The actual scope of the long form report is agreed between the RA, the company's directors and the nomad or sponsor.

Although the report is normally comprehensive, in some circumstances the scope may be restricted, for example where the company floating has not traded (as in a cash shell) or the nomad/sponsor has obtained information from other sources such as commercial due diligence.

The typical contents of a long form report would include:

- business history;

- business operations, including:
  - operational structure
  - company's products and services
  - markets, customers, competition and marketing methods
  - production, facilities and suppliers
  - research and development
  - business premises;
- management and staff;
- financial reporting and management information systems and controls;
- historic financial information;
- tax;
- other matters, eg insurance cover.

The long form report will provide a comprehensive overview of the company and the RA will typically spend two or more weeks on site at the company interviewing management and staff and reviewing documentation, books and records.

The RA will also highlight in the long form report issues that need to be resolved before or after flotation together with proposed solutions. Every company is individual but the types of issue that often arise include:

- inadequate financial reporting and management information systems;
- inappropriate accounting policies;
- concern over items included in the historic financial information, for example irrecoverable debts, obsolete stock, etc;
- tax issues.

The RA will usually communicate significant issues to the directors and the nomad/sponsor as they arise, rather than waiting until the written report is produced. If the work on site is expected to take a number of weeks the RA may also arrange interim meetings to update on progress. Rapid identification of problems so that solutions can be implemented on a timely basis is a key aspect of the RA's work. In extreme cases, if major issues are incapable of resolution it may be necessary to delay or even abort the float and it is important that such issues are identified early before excessive time and costs have been incurred.

Companies often find the long form report a helpful document as this may be the first time that anyone outside the company has spent time reviewing and producing an independent appraisal of it.

Working capital report

The review of forecast financial information is usually included in a separate report to the long form report, although for smaller companies these may be combined. The working capital report has a specific purpose: to provide comfort on the adequacy of working capital, for the reasons explained below.

The directors are required to make a statement on the adequacy of working capital in the investment circular. The wording can vary but is typically along the lines of:

> The directors are of the opinion that, having made due and careful enquiry and after taking into account the placing proceeds[3] and available banking facilities, that the company and its group has sufficient working capital for its present requirements, that is for at least 12 months from the date of this document.

The working capital report is the directors' 'due and careful enquiry'; ie the RA performs procedures to enable the directors to make their working capital statement.

The RA will perform a detailed review of the company's forecast, which must cover at least 12 months from the expected flotation date and preferably up to 18 months. Issues identified in the review, such as errors in the forecast model and unreasonable assumptions will be notified to management so that changes can be made. The final report will include:

- the opinion of the RA that:
  - the forecast is correctly compiled on the basis of the directors' assumptions
  - the forecast is arithmetically accurate
  - the directors have made their working capital statement after due and careful enquiry;

- a summary of the RA's review:
  - results of testing the forecast model and the impact of any unresolved errors on the forecast
  - past forecasting history
  - forecast assumptions and supporting evidence
  - sensitivity testing of key assumptions.

The RA will try hard to resolve issues with the company during the review so that a 'clean' opinion can be given in the report in relation to the directors' statement. If issues cannot be resolved, for example if there is insufficient time to correct an error in the model, then the RA will assess the impact of such errors in coming to their conclusion.

If working capital is clearly inadequate then early identification of this will give time for the company and its advisers to seek additional sources such as bank finance or increased fundraising from the flotation.

Published forecast information

If the company intends to publish forecast information in the investment circular then the working capital report may serve a second purpose and that is to provide comfort on the reasonableness of the forecast figures included in the investment circular.

The RA's work and report will be similar but there will be an increased emphasis on the quality of the forecast information that is being disclosed, and this may involve a more detailed review of the underlying assumptions than is necessary for the level of comfort given on working capital.

OTHER DOCUMENTS

The RA has to produce a multitude of other documents during a flotation. Most of these are short letters providing comfort on various subjects. The following are the more important in terms of the work involved:

- statement of adjustments;

- comfort on financial reporting procedures;
- other financial information in the investment circular;
- material changes.

Statement of adjustments

If the historic financial information in the accountants' report has been changed from the published audited information then a reconciliation is required between the two, showing and explaining what changes have been made. This is referred to as a 'statement of adjustments'; it is prepared by the RA and made publicly available.

Financial reporting procedures

It is important that quoted companies have robust and reliable financial information systems so that accurate information is readily available on a timely basis.

The nomad/sponsor will seek written confirmation from the company along the following lines:

> The directors have established procedures which give a reasonable basis for them to make proper judgements as to the financial position and prospects of the company and its group and are satisfied that this has been given after due and careful enquiry.

As part of the review for the long form report the RA reviews the company's financial and management information systems. One aspect of this review is to enable the RA to confirm that the directors have made their confirmation in relation to procedures 'after due and careful enquiry'. This confirmation is usually included in a separate letter that refers to the work the RA has done in this area in the long form report.

Occasionally current systems and procedures are not adequate for a quoted company and the RA's confirmation may make reference to actions that must be taken within a certain time period and that confirmation is given on the basis that these actions will be complied with.

Other financial information in the investment circular

The investment circular may include financial information outside the sections covered by reports of the RA. A typical example is a summary of key financial data in the 'front end'. The RA will be responsible for checking that this information is correctly extracted from either his or her reports or from the company's records and will provide a letter confirming that this has been done.

Material changes

Material changes in the financial or trading position of the company should be disclosed in the investment circular. The RA will provide a letter confirming that he or she is not aware of any such changes that have not been disclosed. The RA will need to perform specific procedures such as reviewing the latest set of management accounts and talking to directors in order to provide this comfort.

OTHER AREAS

Audit

As discussed earlier, the RA may need to perform audit work on the company, or arrange for it to be performed by another firm.

Re-registration under s43 CA85

A company offering shares to the public must be registered as a plc. Most companies going public are limited companies and so they must re-register; in some cases (eg where the trading company has accumulated losses) a new holding company that is registered as a plc is put in its place.

A company re-registering must obtain a report confirming that it has assets that exceed the total of its share capital and undistributable reserves based on a balance sheet dated within seven months of the re-registration date. This report can be signed by the company's auditors or by the RA.

The RA will need to perform specific procedures in order to give the report and may be able to combine these with the work in other areas. In some cases it may be necessary for a balance sheet to be prepared and audited for the purposes of the re-registration.

The RA will advise the company on what is required and will ensure that the work is performed as necessary.

Tax and other advice

The RA will be able to provide the company with access to a range of services such as advice on tax, share structures, systems implementation and so on. Although such services are not specifically part of the RA's role in a flotation, the RA's knowledge of the company's needs and the services he or she can provide to meet those needs is often invaluable in the flotation process.

Notes

1. The term 'investment circular' is used as a general term for prospectuses and Listing Particulars.
2. References to 'company' also include the company's subsidiary undertakings unless the context indicates otherwise.
3. The cash to be raised on flotation.

11

The role of the corporate broker

Shaun Dobson (Robert W Baird Limited)

INTRODUCTION

The job of the corporate broker is to ensure a successful flotation for the company ('Newco'). A successful flotation means not only achieving an acceptable price for the selling shareholders and company, but also an acceptable price for the new investors – in short, a price that has advantages for both sides.

A flotation takes many months to effect, and involves the company incurring substantial costs, many of which will not be contingent upon success – therefore exposing the company to significant cost risks. It is true to say that there are certain times when the new issue market will not support an issue at the historically conventional price discount of 10 per cent to its quoted peers. Indeed, in the first half of 2002 we saw that discount stretched to up to 25 per cent, reflecting the 'buyers' market' nature of the equity market. At times like this, unless there is an absolute need to come to market (perhaps owing to requiring additional funds to gain first mover advantage), it is often better to wait until better market conditions prevail. This valuation dilemma is exacerbated when significant vendor share sales are envisaged; in recent years we have seen many flotations abandoned because the vendors were unwilling to sell stock at the achievable issue price, rather than a lack of institutional demand being the problem.

In addition to market-related pricing problems, there is also the question as to whether the company is suitable for flotation, which is not solely a regulatory issue but rather one of institutional perception. Certain businesses have been seen by institutional investors as having characteristics that make them unsuitable to be a quoted company, such as a business overly dependent on people (Financial PR agencies being a possible example).

A way of mitigating this risk is to assess the interest that investors might have in the company at a very early stage in the flotation process, ideally before any material costs have been incurred. In effect, the market can be tested prior to a decision to push the flotation button.

This strategy will:

- provide potential investors with an appreciation of the growth potential of Newco;
- increase potential investors' awareness of Newco's performance and prospects; and
- make the specialist fund managers aware of the characteristics of Newco's business.

Test marketing will help the broker give accurate market advice on the institutional perception of Newco before Newco has committed to material expense. This feedback may also raise issues that the broker will have time to address properly in advance of the actual fundraising marketing. Typically, test marketing could comprise a series (perhaps six to eight) of one-to-one presentations with a cross-section of the investment community, in which the presentation will focus exclusively on Newco's business rather than on value and raising funds. The corporate broker will work alongside Newco to draft a presentation showing the merits of Newco's business and its positioning in its marketplace. This presentation provides the written structure for use in the test marketing. This form of test marketing can be of great assistance to the company seeking flotation, as well as giving the shareholders confidence in the likely market appetite for the proposition. The test marketing would be expected to take place three to six months before the actual marketing period commences.

Maximizing the demand for the shares

The key element in maximizing the demand for shares is to create an awareness of Newco amongst relevant institutional investors. A broker will centre his or her approach on the production of a pre-flotation research document, containing a message designed specifically to attract key investment institutions to consider an investment in Newco. In this document the broker will highlight the quality of Newco's business, through a commentary on the principal characteristics and status of Newco, its potential and its markets; and a detailed account of how Newco intends to develop its business and how future success is to be achieved. Typically, this research will not include any forecasts or financial projections but may discuss the growth potential of the relevant market.

Whilst preparation of the pre-flotation research document is being progressed (by the research analyst), work on the prospectus is being continued. Whilst project management of the flotation process and responsibility for the prospectus lie with the sponsor/financial adviser, the corporate broker has significant input into key elements of the document, principally relating to the key marketing themes. This document, which will eventually become the Prospectus, is termed a 'pathfinder' prospectus and is used in the flotation marketing.

In addition to the 'pathfinder' prospectus, the corporate broker will work alongside Newco to draft an institutional presentation. This will again focus on key marketing themes to help persuade would-be investors of the merits of investing in Newco. The presentation typically will also set out the transactions's proposed timing, structure and sometimes valuation.

On the basis of a 'pathfinder' prospectus, Newco will be actively marketed to institutional clients by a specialist sales and research team who are in contact with the institutional investors. This well-proven approach will generate interest in the opportunity to invest in Newco.

Harnessing the demand

Once Newco's profile has been raised within the investment community, the broker will endeavour to convert this interest into a firm commitment to support the flotation by instituting a programme designed to introduce the management of the company to the decision makers at targeted institutions. This will be effected by means of:

- one-to-one meetings with key institutional clients;
- group meetings (including company visits, if appropriate) with a wider selection of institutions;
- an internal presentation to the corporate broker's institutional sales team.

These meetings will be held mainly at the institutional clients' offices, in the broker's own offices and at luncheon venues. The corporate broker will play a major part in the preparation of the presentations, advising on content and the method of delivery. These meetings usually last an hour in total (around 25 minutes for the presentation and the remainder for questions/discussion).

Financial public relations will be an important part of the Newco flotation process and a suitable firm should be appointed as soon as possible. The financial PR agents will be responsible for the arrangement of press and other media releases and interviews both before and after the flotation. They will also be responsible for introducing Newco to a wider audience of financial analysts.

During the programme of presentations the corporate broker will assess the level of demand for Newco shares. This enables the broker to concentrate the marketing programme so as to maximize the level of interest and to make an accurate judgement of the price at which the flotation can be successfully achieved.

Managing a successful flotation aftermarket

As part of the flotation strategy the corporate broker will aim to:

- secure the support of the institutions that make up the inner core of their client-base, who would be the placees of a major part of the issue;
- ensure that those institutions had continuing unsatisfied buying demand after the flotation, which would be used after dealings commenced to absorb any loose stock (this may be achieved by scaling down the amount of stock allocated to each institution, hence leaving them only partially satisfied);
- discuss (in conjunction with the sponsor/financial adviser and Newco) the levels of institutional demand and agree on appropriate new issue price for Newco; this price will be set to ensure that there is an acceptable balance between institutional demand, new issue discount and Newco's aspirations and industry comparables;
- secure an orderly market and implicitly a firm price in the shares by arranging regular institutional visits to Newco, research notes and presentations to ensure the maintenance of the necessary information and awareness.

In recent years the corporate broker has increasingly been involved in the underwriting of a new issue, either in whole or in conjunction with the sponsor/financial adviser. This momentum has largely been driven by the corporate broker being perceived as having the best understanding of the risk involved (as it is closest to the market). In addition, if boutique investment banks and/or accountancy firms act as sponsor (as has recently occurred) they typically do not have a balance sheet which would enable them to underwrite a new issue.

ACTING AS LISTING AGENT

The corporate broker will liaise with the UK Listing Authority (UKLA) or, if appropriate, the AiM team on Newco's behalf to ensure that the flotation prospectus complies with all of the UKLA Listing Rules. They will seek to ensure, through close and long-standing relationships with the Listing Department, that Newco receives the London Stock Exchange's approval for listing in the most efficient and straightforward manner.

Managing the aftermarket

Once Newco has been established as a successful new issue, the role of the broker becomes less intense but remains equally important. Key elements of the continuing role are set out below.

Managing Newco's institutional shareholders

Continuing to develop a broad and stable base of well-informed and supportive institutional shareholders is crucial in assisting Newco to follow its chosen strategy. Close contact between Newco and the corporate broker will be essential to enable production of in-depth research and regular comment on Newco's business. As Newco's appointed stockbroker, the corporate broker will consistently act as the company's interface with the investment community.

To further assist in the management of this process, Newco will have access to regular reports on market movements and relevant news, which will enable Newco to understand in greater detail the significant events affecting the company within the market place, such as:

- which institutions have been buying/selling Newco shares;
- what has been the level of recent market activity in Newco shares;
- what has been the effect on the share price;
- what has caused the movements in the share price;
- which institutions are over-weight or under-represented in their holdings in Newco.

The broker can then use this knowledge within the market place to explain why these events have occurred and to provide suggestions if action is considered to be necessary. This analysis is proactive rather than reactive and helps Newco to manage the relationship with its shareholders.

Thereafter a broker will undertake a continuing marketing role in conjunction with the company to widen the range of institutions that are investors in Newco.

Managing Newco's relationship with the London Stock Exchange

Once Newco becomes a listed company it has to comply with a new set of regulations and will be affected by the ever-changing requirements of the financial markets. The company's corporate stock-broker will keep Newco in regular touch with stock market developments and perceptions which relate to it; and advise Newco on the day-to-day requirements and continuing obligations of a listed company and liaise on the company's behalf with the London Stock Exchange and UKLA.

To assist growth

The corporate broker can assist the growth of Newco in various ways, including:

- raising further capital for the company, as and when sensibly required, by ensuring the necessary support from the market. Support will be created as a result of the continual flow of information between Newco, the broker and institutional investors;
- introducing Newco, as necessary, to the US and European networks of the broker and, if appropriate, to related industrial contacts through this network;
- providing specific proposals for acquisitions, which will be generated by research, corporate finance and mergers and acquisitions activities across the broker's network of offices.

To protect investors

The broker will endeavour to protect investors in Newco by:

- advising the company on the terms on which acquisitions or divestments might be made and the likely resultant impact on Newco shares;
- researching extensively any proposed diversification away from Newco's areas of expertise and/or into new geographical areas;
- ensuring that the marketplace is always adequately apprised of developments at Newco, thereby achieving compliance with Newco's continuing Stock Exchange listing obligations as well as maintaining the confidence and trust of investors at large.

12

Valuing the company's shares

Colin Aaronson (Grant Thornton)

SUMMARY

- A company's valuation will be expressed as a multiple of anticipated earnings. The multiple will usually be based on the P/E
  ratio (price/earnings) of a comparable publicly quoted
  company's shares, discounted to attract investors at flotation.
- The flotation will be considered successful if the offer or placing
  is oversubscribed and, following flotation, the shares start
  trading at a premium to the offer or placing price. Conversely, a
  certain stigma will attach to shares that go to a discount. Within
  reason, brokers will tend to price the issue on the low side, in
  order to ensure that the shares go to a premium.
- Most owner-managers will be selling, at most, a limited number
  of shares when floating a company. The float price will therefore
  affect dilution, which is the proportion of a company the
  owners have to give away to raise a fixed amount of money.

Owners will want the highest possible price to minimize dilution.

- Brokers will set a share price to balance the two conflicting requirements of minimizing dilution while ensuring that the shares go to a premium.

INTRODUCTION

One of the most important questions for any business owner floating a business is, 'How much is my business worth?' Usually, owners will not be selling more than a small percentage of their holdings, but will be creating new shares that will be offered to the public or placed with institutions to raise money for the company. Although the owners are not selling their own shares, they still have to bear a cost, namely 'dilution', which is the percentage of the company the owner has to give up to raise the required funds. The price at which those shares are placed or offered will determine the level of dilution. The higher the float price, the lower the level of dilution.

However, it is important that the shares, when listed, start trading at a premium to the placing or offer price or, at the very least, do not start trading at a discount. If shares go to a premium, the flotation will be regarded as a success, and satisfied investors who have made either a cash or paper profit on their investment will be more likely to take shares in subsequent fundraisings. When shares go to a discount, some of the investors in the placing or offer will try to sell their holdings in the company once the share price reaches the flotation price and they can recoup their investment. This may put a 'lid' on the share price, until those investors have all sold their shares. Once a share trades at a discount, it can take a considerable amount of time for it to trade at above its float price.

The job of setting the price at which the shares are to be placed falls to the broker. The broker has analysts and sales people who have a detailed and up-to-date knowledge of the values being accorded to such businesses by those institutions that are likely to take shares when the company comes to market. The valuation will be based upon the P/E ratios of similar publicly quoted companies, less a percentage to make the shares attractive to investors. There is a potential conflict of interest between the broker and its client company. While the broker's commission will be maximized by a higher price, it will tend to favour a price at the lower end of a possible range in order to make the fundraising process relatively easy and to ensure, as far as possible, that the shares start trading at a premium. The company's owners will generally prefer a higher price to minimize dilution. An independent adviser – a nominated adviser or a sponsor – can help to ensure a fair balance between these conflicting demands.

However, a company coming to market may have a number of different types of businesses, or 'income streams', which means that the company can actually be compared to a number of different quoted companies, operating in different sectors, each of which has a significantly different P/E ratio. It may even not have earnings upon which to calculate a valuation, or may not be directly comparable to quoted companies. Where there are different income streams, the business can be analysed and each part of the company valued separately.

The P/E ratios reflect market consensus, but they also imply a valuation that is based on rational principles.

THE PRINCIPLES OF VALUATION

Any investment decision, whether it be a quoted investment or plant and machinery, is based on a comparison of the cost of an investment with the benefits deriving from that investment, whether it is in the form of cost savings or interest or dividend income. The income from a quoted investment comes in the form of dividends, and capital growth that can be realized when the investor sells the shares. However, as the market value of a company at any time reflects the present value of anticipated dividend streams, all other things being equal, capital growth equates to anticipated dividend growth.

The dividend valuation model

Investors valuing a business on the basis of future dividends calculate the present value of those dividends, that is the value to them *now* of those future dividends. The present value of those cash flows is the nominal value of each dividend discounted back to the present day at an appropriate discount rate. If, for example, the discount rate was 10 per cent, and a dividend of £10,000 was anticipated in one year's time, the present value would be:

£10,000/1.1 = £9,091

The same dividend in two years' time would today be worth:

£10,000/(1.1)² = £8,265

A dividend of £10,000 received in perpetuity would have a present value of:

£10,000/0.1 = £100,000

What discount rate?

The discount rate reflects the alternative returns available (such as bank interest), and takes account of the inherent risk in an equity investment. It will therefore be considerably higher than the government bond rate or another investment that is for practical purposes risk-free.

In practice however, the discount rate of a company implied by its forecast profits and its market capitalization can be close to or even lower than the bank rate of interest. This is because it takes account of growth. If growth in dividends is assumed to be constant, then the value of a company can be calculated as:

$V = D_1/(r-g)$, where:

V   is the value of the business;

D_1 is the expected dividend in one year's time, usually based on the company's own forecasts;

r   is the required rate of return; and

g   is the expected rate of growth in dividends.

If, for example, a company was expecting to pay a dividend of £10,000 in a year's time, the required rate of return is 10 per cent and the anticipated growth rate is 7.5 per cent, then the business will be valued at:

$$£10,000 / (0.1 - 0.075) = £400,000$$

In the above example, the valuation of £400,000 implies a discount rate of 2.5 per cent. By factoring in growth in this example, discount rates can appear to be lower than the bank interest rate.

Growth itself can be estimated in three ways:

1.   from companies' forecasts, or brokers' estimates for similar companies;
2.   extrapolating from past growth;
3.   by applying the company's return on capital employed (ROCE) to its retained profits.

Determining the required rate of return

In discussing the discount rate, so far we have assumed a required rate of return and have adjusted it to take account of growth. The discount rate can also be adjusted to take account of taxation and other complicating factors.

What determines the required rate of return, or more precisely, what determines the risk premium, which is the additional return that compensates investors for the risk they face in investing in a business? One method of determining the required rate of return for an (as yet) private company, and thereby calculating the risk premium, is to find a comparative quoted company, and to calculate the implied rate of return based on brokers' forecasts and the share price. A similar calculation can be made for a market sector, or for the market as a whole.

An alternative approach, and one that is arguably more rigorous, is to use the Capital Asset Pricing Model (CAPM). CAPM calculates the required rate of return as:

$r = r^f + \beta(r^m - r^f)$, where:

r^f is the risk-free rate of return, which equates to the rate of return on government stock;

r^m is the rate of return of the stock market as a whole, and

β is the perceived level of the company's risk, relative to the market. It takes account of the volatility of earnings and the level of gearing. A β value of 0 implies zero risk, a β value of 1 implies a level of risk typical of the market as a whole, and a β value greater than 1 implies a company with a higher than average level of perceived risk. β values for a company can be measured empirically by comparing past movements in returns with movements in the market return. In addition, the London Business School's Institute of Finance and Accounting offers a Risk Measurement Service that provides β values for major publicly listed companies.

If for example the rate of interest on gilts was 5 per cent, and the rate of return required of the stock market as a whole was 20 per cent, for a company with a β value of 2 (twice the average level of risk), the required return will be:

$5\% + 2 \times (20\% \text{ less } 5\%) = 35\%$

Asset-based valuations

A business can be seen as a collection of assets, whose value is based on the company's audited balance sheet. While an asset-based valuation may be useful or appropriate for an asset-based business such as a property company, for most companies it is largely irrelevant for the following reasons:

- it is based on accounting policies the choice of which may be subjective;
- accounts are drawn up on a going concern basis; balance sheet values are not based on values that would be achieved in a break-up situation;
- it may not deal adequately with intangible assets, particularly brand values, goodwill and intellectual property rights.

Publications such as the *Investors Chronicle* do compare companies' share prices to the value of the company's underlying net assets, but the fact that the two valuations are usually quite different emphasizes the irrelevance, in most cases, of net asset value to a company's market capitalization.

However, asset values can underpin the market value of a company, particularly if balance sheet values do not fully reflect the realizable value of certain assets. This may be relevant if a company has significant property assets that have not been revalued for a number of years.

A company's assets are valuable to the extent that they enable the company to trade and to generate profits. Their value to a business is the value of the cash that those assets generate. For most investors, that cash flow takes the form of dividends.

VALUATION IN PRACTICE

Brokers' analysts are able to perform highly sophisticated calculations to determine the value of a business based on anticipated growth, dividends, and an appropriate discount rate. In practice however, the analysts will compare a business to a similar quoted company, and apply that company's P/E ratio to the earnings of the business.

P/E ratios reflect the market's expectations of growth. On 31 August 2002, the mining sector had the lowest sector P/E ratio of 9.33, whereas one of the highest, telecommunications services, had a P/E greater than 50. This implies that the market expects faster growth in the latter sector, but P/E ratios can also be affected by reduced short-term profits.

A company can be growing faster than its peer group, and this will affect the valuation accorded to it. Faster growth may be a reflection of stronger and more dynamic management, or of the stage of development of the business. If growth is perceived to be the result of strong management, that will enhance the company's valuation.

Valuation can be affected by other factors:

- Selecting the appropriate sector can make a significant difference. On 10 June 2002, the engineering and machinery sector had an average P/E ratio of 16, whereas the support services sector had an average P/E of almost 22. A company that provided services to engineering and other companies would probably achieve a higher valuation if investors were to perceive it as a support service rather than an engineering business. A company cannot be portrayed as something it is not, but there is some flexibility, and perhaps a lesson for strategy.
- Within a company, there could be a number of different income streams, each of which could be valued differently.
- If a company is growing, other things being equal it will generally achieve a higher valuation if it delays flotation, thereby reporting higher profits on which a P/E will be based.
- Market sentiment changes over time, and is crucial in determining both the price at which shares are offered, and indeed whether the fundraising will succeed at all. Market sentiment can therefore both amplify and negate the effect of delaying flotation (referred to in the previous point) on the flotation price.

The value that analysts give to a company will influence investors but, ultimately, can only be indicative. The price that investors are prepared to pay for a company's stock (and hence that company's valuation) will be determined either informally through discussions, or from formal responses to a 'pathfinder' prospectus.

Valuation techniques such as the dividend valuation model discussed above may be used to support a valuation, but the valuation of a private company will be based upon a comparable quoted company. Even where there is no direct equivalent, analysts will find a quoted company that can be used as a basis of comparison.

Where a company is forecasting profits growth, the credibility of the forecast profits and the extent to which they form the basis of a valuation will depend on a number of factors, including:

- the experience and perceived quality of management;
- track record;
- 'visibility' of earnings (the extent to which forecast earnings are underpinned by contracts or supported by trading history);
- the quality of advisers and the brokers' relationship with their institutional clients.

13

Tax planning for the company and the shareholders

Robert Langston (Grant Thornton)

TAX ISSUES FOR THE COMPANY

Due diligence

As part of the due diligence process, prospective investors will want to be assured that the company is not exposed to:

- unknown tax liabilities;
- unpaid tax liabilities;
- interest on unpaid tax liabilities;
- penalties for failing to pay tax;
- penalties for failing to make necessary returns to the Inland Revenue;
- tax liabilities arising as a result of the transaction.

It is therefore normal practice for appropriate tax specialists to be fully involved in a due diligence review. Areas subject to review will include:

- corporation tax returns;
- corporation tax payments;
- transactions with related overseas companies;
- necessary claims and elections;
- payroll;
- benefits in kind;
- VAT;
- Stamp Duty.

The prospectus will usually provide comfort that tax due diligence has been undertaken, and that there are no outstanding liabilities of the type outlined above.

Restructuring prior to the float

Although perhaps more common with larger floats, it may be that not all of the activities of a company are destined for the stock market. Assets and trading activities may have to be split between the company (or group) that is being floated, and another company (or group) that is to remain in private hands.

Equally, assets or trading activities may be split between various parallel companies (ie companies not in the same group, but with common shareholders) and an amalgamation will be necessary prior to the float.

Although there are many ways in which these objectives can be achieved, the most usual are:

- a demerger via dividends in specie;
- liquidation under s110 Insolvency Act 1986;
- a disposal of assets from one company to another (for cash or debt);
- a disposal of assets from one company to another (for shares).

Of course there are tax consequences to each of these methods and liabilities will have to be managed at both the time of restructuring and the float itself.

Generally speaking, the disposal of a chargeable asset by a company to a person other than another company that is a member of the same group will give rise to a chargeable gain subject to corporation tax. Chargeable assets include most fixed assets, but not:

- cash;
- stock;
- debtors;
- plant and machinery where both the cost and disposal proceeds are below £6,000.

(This list is not exhaustive.)

From 1 April 2002, an exemption from corporation tax on chargeable gains is available for the disposal of substantial shareholdings provided that a number of conditions are satisfied. This allows qualifying subsidiary companies to be sold from groups free from corporation tax prior to flotation.

Transfers of assets between companies in the same group do not give rise to a chargeable gain, and therefore no corporation tax liability arises. However, if the transferee company leaves the group within six years of the transfer an exit charge arises. This charge will be equal to the gain that would arise on a sale of the asset at its market value at the time of the original intra-group transfer. This will in many cases give rise to a chargeable gain and therefore a corporation tax liability.

From 1 April 2002, it is possible to elect that this charge instead arises in a company that is a member of the same group as the transferee company at the time of leaving the group. This may allow capital losses to be utilized against the exit charge. Also from 1 April 2002 it is possible to defer this exit charge under the rollover relief provisions if investment is made into a 'qualifying asset' within the specified time period. Qualifying assets include land and property and fixed plant and machinery that are used for the purposes of a trade.

Despite the new substantial shareholding exemption, tax charges can therefore arise in respect of asset transfers between group companies when a company (or subgroup of companies) leaves a group, for instance where a subsidiary is spun out from a group prior to floating that group, or a parent company floats a subsidiary and the new issue of shares leads to the subsidiary ceasing to be a member of the parent's group.

For the purposes of chargeable gains (there are other definitions for other purposes), a group of companies comprises a 'principal company' and any of its subsidiaries that are owned at least 75 per cent by their immediate parent company, or are owned (indirectly) more than 50 per cent by the principal company.

Transfers between companies may bear a Stamp Duty liability – though group relief is available for transfers within a group. However, the Finance Act 2002 introduces a claw back of Stamp Duty 'group' relief, broadly where the company into which UK real estate has been transferred leaves the group within two years of the transfer.

Demerger

More complicated pre-float reconstructions may involve the issue of shares by new companies to existing shareholders, followed by a transfer of assets or shares in a subsidiary to this new company.

To ensure that chargeable gains do not arise on this transfer of assets, relief is available under s139 Taxation of Chargeable Gains Act (TCGA) 1992. Provided certain conditions are satisfied, the transfer of assets will not give rise to a chargeable gain. A similar relief is available under s136 TCGA to ensure that the shareholders in the transferor company do not realize a capital gain when they are issued with shares in the new company.

The transfers of assets and shares between companies on a pre-float reconstruction may give rise to Stamp Duty liabilities (at 0.5 per cent for shares, and up to 4 per cent for other assets – mainly UK real estate and debtors/creditors). However, reliefs are available in restrictive circumstances to exempt certain transfers, including the transfer of shares to a new holding company (s77 Finance Act 1986), and the transfer of an undertaking in exchange for shares as part of a reconstruction (most commonly on a demerger).

The exemptions must be adjudicated with the Stamp Office, and the shareholdings of the recipient companies must be the same as those in the target company.

VAT issues on restructuring

Changing the way that shares are owned (including the flotation itself) may change the VAT registration – particularly where group registrations are involved. Changing the ownership of assets will involve transactions which are, potentially, subject to VAT; and where the assets involved are land and property particular care is required to ensure this does not involve an unnecessary cost.

Even where property is not involved, changing the structure of a business, for example by hiving off different operations into different companies, or creating a management company, is likely to create transactions that did not exist previously and, in many cases, these transactions will be subject to VAT. Care is needed to ensure that this does not create unnecessary VAT costs – for example, if the recipient of those transactions cannot reclaim VAT that the supplier is required to charge.

Clearances

An integral part of managing the tax liabilities on a float involve obtaining clearance from the Inland Revenue that it will not seek to charge tax under the anti-avoidance provisions of s703 ICTA 1988. Broadly speaking, s703 charges tax on 'transactions in securities' (which could include a float) where a 'tax advantage' has been obtained. The Inland Revenue is increasingly seeking to charge tax under this section, and looks out for particular transactions, such as those involving payments of cash to shareholders who will retain control, or to minority shareholders who are members of their family.

Clearance under s707 ICTA 1988 should always be obtained on a float to protect against any possible charge under s703 and to provide comfort to incoming shareholders. Other clearances may be necessary if prior reconstructions have taken place (for instance if relief has been claimed under s136 or s139), and the prospectus will usually provide comfort that all necessary tax clearances have been obtained.

In any case, the Inland Revenue has a time limit of 30 days from the date of application in order to give clearance. If it requires further information or particulars, the time limit is extended to 30 days from the date on which this further information is provided. It is therefore prudent to apply for tax clearance 60 days before the scheduled date of the float.

VAT recovery on costs

Preparing a business to go public, and the float itself, will involve costs of which some, if not most, will bear VAT. Because flotation involves the issue or sale of shares (which are exempt from VAT) it may not be possible to reclaim this VAT from Customs & Excise. Therefore, this extra cost needs to be factored in when budgeting for the float. However, with careful planning and negotiation with Customs & Excise the potential VAT costs can be reduced considerably.

TAX ISSUES FOR THE SHAREHOLDERS

Flotation brings with it a number of indirect, but very important, consequences for tax purposes:

- the Inland Revenue's method of share valuation tends to deflate the value of unquoted shares against quoted shares and so, for tax purposes, the value of shares will immediately increase;
- the availability of many tax reliefs depends on the quoted status of shares (see later);
- some shareholdings may be diluted following the float so that they no longer qualify for certain tax reliefs.

It is therefore important for shareholders to consider tax planning prior to a float in order to take advantage not only of tax reliefs, but also of the low values placed on unquoted shares for tax purposes.

Planning measures to consider prior to a float include:

- make any intended gifts (or other disposals) to minimize any potential capital gains tax and corresponding tax liability (gifts of unquoted shares may also qualify for CGT holdover relief – see below);
- gifts to low- or non-taxpayers will ensure that future dividends are taxed at lower rates of tax (any capital gains made on future sales of shares will also be taxed at lower rates);
- a transfer into a trust may also allow future dividends and gains to be taxed at a lower rate of tax, and use of an appropriate trust can be more flexible than an outright gift; shareholders contemplating this will also need to consider how their entitlement to taper relief may be affected;
- rather than taking advantage of reliefs, triggering a taxable disposal prior to the float may take advantage of tax reliefs that will not be available after the float; in many cases a gift to a family member or a trust will be the easiest way to achieve this objective;
- in addition, reliefs may simply be withdrawn by the government following the float – for instance, retirement relief will not be available for disposals of shares after 5 April 2003, and a common planning measure is to trigger a taxable gain by settling shares onto a trust (trusts created for this purpose are known colloquially as 'retirement relief trusts').

Some transfers may be dictated by commercial considerations if some of the assets (or goodwill) of the business are not held directly by the company or group that is being floated. Although these transfers may be unavoidable, it is still important to structure them correctly so that unnecessary tax liabilities do not arise.

There are three important tax reliefs:

1. If assets already used in the trade are gifted or sold at under value to the company, holdover relief may be available under s165 TCGA 1992 to defer any capital gain until the company eventually sells the asset.

2. In addition to a capital gain, a balancing allowance may arise on the transfer of an industrial building – representing the claw back of any industrial buildings allowances already given; an election can be made to avoid this if the two parties to the transaction are connected.
3. If relief under s165 is not available, or the assets are transferred at market value, the gain can still be deferred if the transferor acquires a new 'qualifying asset' within a period beginning one year before and ending three years after the transfer. Qualifying assets include land and property and fixed plant and machinery that are used for a trade.

For Stamp Duty, transfers of assets to companies can trigger unexpected liabilities. If UK real estate is transferred by a shareholder to a connected company, then there is a deemed market value consideration, charged at up to 4 per cent. Thankfully, transfers of goodwill or intellectual property are now exempt from Stamp Duty, but the transfer of certain other assets (debtors and benefits of contracts/work in progress) requires care.

One final point to consider when undertaking pre-float planning is that the Inland Revenue often takes the view that for valuation purposes, shares can take on their quoted value before they are actually quoted, for instance when:

-   the directors agree that the float will take place;
-   knowledge of the planned float becomes public;
-   the prospectus is issued.

This means that it is important to undertake planning as early as possible when considering a float.

For the purposes of establishing whether they qualify for the particular tax reliefs, shares remain unquoted until they are actually quoted.

14

Indemnities and warranties from directors and shareholders

Philip Goldsborough (Pinsent Curtis Biddle)

INTRODUCTION

This chapter considers the warranties and indemnities generally given in the context of a flotation and, more specifically, those contained in an underwriting agreement.

The underwriting agreement is one of the principal documents that will be entered into in connection with the underwriting of shares on a flotation. The principal purpose of the underwriting agreement is to:

- define the obligations of the issuing house to the company and the selling shareholders in its capacity as underwriter;
- provide the issuing house with protection against potential liabilities from third parties;

- assist the issuing house in satisfying certain of its duties as sponsor and maintaining an orderly market in the shares post flotation.

FUNCTION OF WARRANTIES AND INDEMNITIES

Invariably, an underwriting agreement will include a series of warranties and a tax indemnity as well as an all-embracing indemnity in favour of the issuing house. Much time can be spent by lawyers advising on a flotation negotiating the terms of these provisions. It is important to consider the function of these warranties and indemnities and what they achieve (or perhaps more importantly, do not achieve).

The company and its directors will normally be requested to warrant that the prospectus complies with the requirements of the Listing Rules and Part IV of the Financial Services Act 1986 (shortly to be replaced by the Financial Services and Markets Act 2000) and to give numerous specific warranties regarding such matters as the accounts, the absence of litigation and sufficiency of working capital.

In the context of an underwriting agreement, these warranties have a three-fold purpose. The first is to act as a sort of checklist for the benefit both of the company and its directors as well as the issuing house so as to concentrate the minds of all those involved on the principal issues that ought to have been addressed in the preparation of the prospectus. The second is to act as a trigger mechanism for termination rights that are normally vested in the issuing house under the terms of the underwriting agreement. The underwriting agreement will normally provide that if any of the warranties are discovered to have been inaccurate or misleading at any time prior to commencement of dealings, or become so during that time, the issuing house may terminate the agreement and thus pull the issue. The third purpose of warranties, but one that is most commonly misunderstood, is as a method of loss recovery.

Loss recovery

In the context of the underwriting of securities, the giving of warranties is something of a blunt instrument as a means of loss recovery. The ability to recover damages for breach of warranty will depend upon the plaintiff satisfying the various hurdles that the common law places before a person who wishes to recover damages for contractual misrepresentation. A person seeking to bring a claim for breach of warranty is required to demonstrate that he or she has suffered loss in consequence of the breach, that the extent and nature of the loss suffered was sufficiently foreseeable and that he or she took reasonable steps to mitigate that loss. In fact, it will often be the case that the issuing house itself has suffered no loss at all, in that all of the securities that were underwritten have been passed to sub-underwriters who have themselves suffered loss by means of a diminution in the value of their securities but who have no direct ability to claim under the warranties. (However, they may have a right to compensation under the Financial Services Act, although this is not certain.)

Various attempts have been made in the past to bridge the gap between the person who has suffered loss (for example, the sub-underwriters) and the person who has received the benefit of the warranties (the issuing house). One possibility is to state that the benefit of the warranties is taken by the issuing house as trustee for the sub-underwriters. Even if this is effective as a matter of law to allow the issuing house to bring an action for loss suffered by the sub-underwriters, characterizing the issuing house as trustee imposes fiduciary obligations on the issuing house that may add to its own liabilities vis-à-vis sub-underwriters.

An alternative possibility is for the issuing house to argue that, since the warrantors would always have foreseen that any loss suffered would be suffered by third parties with whom securities were sub-underwritten, the issuing house should be able to recover the loss of those third parties.

An issuing house may prefer simply to ensure that the under-writing agreement includes a well-drafted indemnity in favour of the issuing house so that the issuing house would be able to recover losses incurred by virtue of actions brought against it by third parties, including sub-underwriters. Unlike a warranty, an indemnity is an express agreement that, should the issuing house suffer loss of a particular nature, the indemnifier will meet those losses. An action brought under such an indemnity does not constitute an action for damages and would not therefore be liable to the various common law rules described above.

In the context of most underwriting agreements, the more important purposes which the warranties serve are that they provide a mechanism for enabling the issuing house to terminate its underwriting obligations, and they focus the minds of those persons giving the warranties (probably more so than verification notes) and thereby act as a further means of due diligence / verification to ensure that the prospectus complies with the statutory requirements.

Sponsor's indemnity

The most important protective provision in the underwriting agreement, so far as the issuing house is concerned, is the 'sponsor's indemnity'. This is an indemnity in favour of the issuing house against loss that it may suffer in connection with the flotation, for example as a result of an investor bringing proceedings against the issuing house alleging that the prospectus did not comply with the general disclosure requirements of section 146 of the Financial Services Act 1986 or was otherwise misleading or inaccurate. The indemnity is not likely to cover loss to the extent that it arises as a result of the issuing house's own negligence or wilful default, or its failure to comply with the rules of the Securities and Futures Authority or other relevant SRO.

There is an ongoing debate at present between practitioners over whether or not the sponsor's indemnity to the extent given by the company may contravene the financial assistance provisions of section 151 of the Companies Act 1985.

WHO GIVES THE WARRANTIES AND THE SPONSOR'S INDEMNITY?

The question of who is to give warranties and the sponsor's indemnity is often the subject of extensive negotiations. The candidates are the company, its directors (both executive and non-executive) and the shareholders. Even though the company may give the warranties and the indemnity, in practice any claim against the company is likely to prejudice the company's new shareholders and the issuing house will therefore prefer to look elsewhere in order to pursue a claim.

The issuing house is likely to insist on the executive directors giving the warranties and indemnity. It may, however, take a less stringent attitude towards the non-executive directors, especially if they have had only a very limited involvement with the company or if they have only recently been appointed to the board (which is frequently the case in the context of flotations). The directors of the company will, in any event, be persons responsible for the prospectus under section 146 of the Financial Services Act 1986 and it is often questioned why they should give contractual undertakings to the issuing house in addition to incurring statutory responsibility.

Whether or not 'non-director' shareholders may be required to be party to warranties and indemnities will differ according to the circumstances of each case. However, it is apparent that institutional shareholders, such as venture capitalists, are simply not prepared to expose themselves to a liability under these circumstances. Indeed, some profess that it would be contrary to their constitution to do so.

TAX INDEMNITY

As part of the protection obtained for the benefit of investors on a flotation, the issuing house will seek a tax indemnity in favour of the company and its subsidiaries. This will either form part of the underwriting agreement or be a separate document. The issuing house will usually look to all or some of the shareholders to give such an indemnity.

In the past it was not unusual for the issuing house to obtain a full tax indemnity, very similar to the type given on the purchase of a private company's shares, to the effect that the company would be indemnified against any charge to tax not provided for in the last audited accounts save as arose in the ordinary course of trading since the last balance sheet date. The current trend, however, is for the issuing house to seek a more limited form of tax indemnity. The rationale is that investors must accept the risk of tax charges that arise in the ordinary course of the company's business and, in any event, the investors may have various statutory and common law remedies if a material liability has not been disclosed.

The more limited types of indemnity will cover tax liabilities that are primarily those of some other person but for which the company has a secondary liability (for example, non-deducted PAYE). The indemnity may also cover the impact of anti-avoidance legislation and certain other liabilities that arise from events not in the ordinary course of the company's trading activities.

Whichever form of indemnity is given, it will usually cover all relevant liabilities up to and including admission to listing of the company's shares.

The issuing house will normally be a party to the indemnity, in addition to the company, in order to be able to enforce the indemnity for the benefit of the company.

LIMITATION ON LIABILITIES

No limitation on the liabilities of the company under the underwriting agreement is likely to be acceptable to the issuing house and, until relatively recently, the same was true for directors and selling shareholders. However, it has become more common for there to be some forms of limitation for the directors (despite the fact that directors' statutory liability under the Financial Services Act is unlimited) and, if applicable, selling shareholders in relation to both the underwriting agreement and the tax indemnity.

The most important limitation is a monetary cap on the total exposure of each of the directors (and selling shareholders). Ultimately, this is a matter of negotiation. However, the following comments may be helpful.

Non-executive directors. The limit here is often calculated by reference to the annual fees that the director will receive as a non-executive director of the company. Two or three times the applicable directors' fees appears to be common, reflecting the different role the non-executive director is expected to play.

Executive directors and selling shareholders. There is no particular common practice here but the cap is not infrequently calculated by reference to the value of the particular person's shareholding in the company.

Putting a time limit on the period within which the issuing house can bring a claim is another way of limiting exposure under the underwriting agreement and tax indemnity. Issuing houses are usually prepared to accept some form of time limit for bringing claims against directors and shareholders (but not the company). Commonly, issuing houses will concede that a claim must be brought against such persons within two or three accounting periods after admission, or six or seven accounting periods in relation to tax matters.

A further form of limitation for the directors which is finding mixed reaction amongst issuing houses is to provide that the issuing house will not be able to claim under the sponsor's indemnity or for breach of warranty against an individual director if that director can show that he or she would have had a defence to such a claim under section 151 of the Financial Services Act 1986, if such claim had been made against him or her under that Act. The rationale for this is that a higher standard of care should not be imposed upon a director than that required of him or her by statute.

RIGHTS OF CONTRIBUTION

Whenever warranties and indemnities are given by more than one person (either jointly, severally or jointly and severally) those persons will (unless there is agreement to the contrary) have a right of contribution against one another in respect of any claim that is made against any of them under those warranties and indemnities (see Civil Liability (Contributions) Act 1978). Therefore, if, say, a claim is made by an issuing house against a director under the sponsor's indemnity and that indemnity has also been given by the other directors and the company, the director against whom the claim is made will be entitled to a contribution from the other directors and the company unless there is express provision to the contrary.

As has been mentioned previously, the issuing house will not wish to make a claim against the company except as a last resort. Similarly, it would not want any of the directors to seek a right of contribution against the company. From the issuing house's point of view therefore, it is desirable that the underwriting agreement should expressly exclude any such right of contribution against the company, although the issuing house will probably not be so concerned about a right of contribution between the directors.

The Civil Liability (Contributions) Act 1978 provides that the amount of contribution to which a person is entitled under that Act is whatever the court decides is just and equitable having regard to the extent of the particular person's responsibility for the damage in question. There is therefore no certainty over the quantum of any contribution that a director may be required to make. The directors should, consequently, consider whether they wish to enter into a separate contribution agreement so that any liability incurred by any of them is shared in the proportions agreed between them (irrespective of any particular director's culpability). Such agreements are permissible under the Act.

15

The role of corporate public relations

Peter Binns (Binns & Co)

Going public is a major milestone in a company's development and is usually a once in a lifetime event. It will impact public awareness, change perceptions about the company's corporate identity, brand build, spur the management team and, if handled correctly, give incentive to the entire workforce.

Most prospectuses and press releases announcing details of flotation read the same: Company X is seeking a listing, 'to help increase its credibility, raise its profile, enhance its status and provide more access to capital', adding, 'and to assist in staff recruitment and employee retention through the ability to offer share options'.

As a vital and, in some cases, logical stage in a company's corporate strategy, a flotation will achieve a number of objectives: it will increase the value of a business, it will strengthen the group's balance sheet, it will broaden the shareholding base, and it will raise new funds for growth.

While a flotation may not immediately raise additional monies, it achieves three important steps for a company:

1. It establishes a rating for a business within its peer group.
2. It facilitates corporate activity.
3. It provides greater flexibility than may be possible for a privately-owned organization.

Above all, it puts a business on a bigger stage, often for the first time, and into the public domain – placing it under greater scrutiny than it has ever experienced from what may seem strange, new and demanding audiences. These include the likes of institutional and retail investors, fund managers and broker analysts, intermediaries, market makers and the media.

Reputations can be won and lost in minutes in the public arena. Without question, publicly listed companies are more newsworthy than privately run concerns and, from the outset, new rules and guidelines need to be established – both in preparation for flotation and for dealing with a new tradable commodity: a publicly quoted share price.

Going public is akin to a battle campaign. It needs to be well planned and well coordinated, with the PR advisory team working closely with the company's presentation team, its financial adviser, its sponsor and its other corporate advisers. As the London Stock Exchange says in its documentation and rules about flotation:

> You should consider carefully the issues involved in joining the world's most international stock market. Such a decision brings responsibilities as well as benefits. You, your board members and your employees must be ready to accept the disciplines inherent in having shares traded publicly and in having outside shareholders whose interests must be taken into account.
>
> In particular, you must be aware that flotation on a public market brings with it the uncertainty of market conditions. Your company's share price may be affected by a number of factors beyond its control, including economic conditions or developments in the same sector.
>
> A further change to bear in mind is that flotation will inevitably lead to closer scrutiny of your company, its performance and its directors. In general, the board must be prepared for greater exposure and openness, in terms of the company's finances and business strategy and in promptly announcing new developments, both positive and negative.

> Keeping investors informed about your company is crucial if your business is to reap the maximum potential benefit from being publicly quoted. Investor relations activities can help increase demand for your shares and ensure that your flotation is as successful as possible, both for the company and its shareholders.

The key to achieving a successful initial public offering (IPO), subject to market conditions and timing, is to build a supportive following among potential investors and opinion-formers and manage the flow of relevant information. An action programme that runs in tandem with the marketing campaign of the IPO's sponsor needs to be established.

A flotation campaign, broadly, falls into three phases:

1. Pre-flotation – concentrating heavily on preparation work, education and profile building.
2. Flotation – addressing the actual sale of the shares and establishing a following.
3. Post-flotation – fostering the development of an active market in the shares.

When to start? It is best to allow adequate forward planning, starting at least two months ahead of Impact Day. If an IPO is capitalized at over £1 billion and is being marketed in several countries, it is best to start six months ahead of Impact Day.

The first step is to agree with the sponsor which *other* brokers should be introduced to Company X *before* Impact Day. While the sponsors manage, price and sell the issue, the marketplace may want an objective view, and 'independent' investment research will be published by other leading firms ahead of or around the time of the pathfinder or the prospectus. This research will be sent to the institutions, the market makers and the press. It may also be sent to and appear on the Multex System, a global provider of investment information that offers investors more than 1 million investment reports from over 400 international brokerage firms and independent research houses. Users of the Multex service range from Reuters and the *Wall Street Journal* to Merrill Lynch, Scottish Widows and individual private investors.

The public relations ('PR') team should first research and approach the appropriate investment analysts, agreeing with the sponsor as to how many firms will be given access to the company's management team ahead of Impact Day, either on a one-to-one basis or by way of a joint briefing.

Next comes the pathfinder and then the prospectus. While this is drafted by all parties, the appointed professional financial PR consultants provide input into the early summary and introduction pages and submit comments on the rest of the text.

Every investor has definite views on the price they are willing to pay for an IPO. Management must also be realistic and adhere to the judgement and experience of their advisers in setting the agenda and the tone for the marketing of the shares.

Whether a company is listing on AiM, the Official List, Nasdaq, the New York Stock Exchange, European Bourse or other stock exchanges worldwide, investors have clear views on the level and content they expect from the presentations. They are cynical (and they can be difficult). They have seen management teams and companies come and go. Often, it may come down to chemistry.

Every presentation should be logical in its format and theme. It should simplify the messages. It *must* be accurate and concise. It needs to be well presented and put across in 15 minutes. The appointed PR firm should help draft, produce and critique the presentation, which will be given at the time of the launch of the pathfinder or the announcement of intention to float.

PRE-FLOTATION

An experienced PR firm will work closely with the company's other advisers to ensure that the media, stockbrokers' analysts and prospective investors, both professional and private, have a clear understanding of a company's business, its culture, its potential and its vision for the future.

It is the PR's job to identify a company's unique selling points in relation to its business, sector and route of flotation and agree a positioning statement that should be common to all communications and serve as the company's recognizable signature.

Preparatory work should also include prospectus design, the creation of a brochure or information pack, a Website, photography, the generation of slide or video presentations, media training and dress rehearsals (the latter two of which are held by journalists with extensive print and broadcasting experience).

FLOTATION

Concurrent to this, the PR devises a media contact programme to achieve maximum impact for the IPO. Every flotation is individual and requires a tailored approach. For instance, the appointed PR firm may recommend a general press announcement at the outset or, alternatively, an exclusive with one newspaper, followed up by an 'intention to list' release. This must be made at least 10 days before the start of trading in your company's shares.

The release could be followed by a mix of further feature coverage prior to the issue of pathfinder and formal publication of the flotation details. All coverage should be carefully targeted, drawing on an extensive range of contacts within the national daily and Sunday press, international media, and the investment magazines, newsletters, online investment sites, wire agencies and broadcasting worlds.

The media programme must be carefully aligned with the organization of institutional investor introductions and briefings with analysts. The build-up of a broad base of analyst support is crucial to the long-term health of the shares and helps the efforts of the company sponsor and broker.

Newsworthiness and overall interest again come down to simple criteria: the size and the route of an IPO. Greater attention will be given by all of the target audiences to an offer for sale than to a subscription, an introduction or a placing. But an IPO is news, even against the likes of over 500 competing stories a day and many thousands weekly.

News of the flotation should be distributed to every relevant audience and either the sponsor or the PR consultant should effect introductions to the likely market makers in the shares, whose number are subject to the size of the issue and availability of stock in the marketplace.

A typical outline flotation timetable is shown in Table 15.1.

Table 15.1 *A typical outline flotation timetable*

Timing	Research/prospectus production/presentation/institutions/ analysts/the media/market makers
2–6 months before flotation	Research: establish appetite for shares amongst institutions/analysts. Position the company. Advise on drafts of prospectus. Design and editing of prospectus. Presentation/media training. Coverage in national and trade press. Participation in industry features/surveys
Announcement of the intention to float	Exclusive with national newspaper. Press release distributed to wire agencies, news services, evenings, nationals, financial onlines, TV, radio, magazines, trades. Design and editing of prospectus cover. Coverage
Pathfinder/marketing commences	Presentation to institutions/possible site visit(s). Analyst presentation(s)/site visit(s). Meet the market makers
Impact Day	Press release/prospectus distributed to City and press. Coverage
First day of dealings Long-term PR campaign	Market reports in national press Agree with company and financial adviser

RUN-UP TO IMPACT DAY

Effective post-flotation support plays an important part in building momentum, ensuring an active after-market in a company's shares and turnover levels that encourage further broker interest and support. The PR professionals liaise closely with the company's other advisers, monitor the company's share price and movements on its share register, and provide regular feedback from the media and the market after publication of results and transactions.

THE AFTER-MARKET

A successful flotation is the platform for a long-term media and investor relations programme involving continuous news and issue management and a broadening of the shareholder base through regular investor, broker and media introductions.

A one-off burst of publicity on the day of flotation will not be sufficient to ensure a proper awareness of a business nor an active after-market in a company's shares. Forward planning, a regular presence and continued support are vital.

Part III

Living with the listing

16

Continuing obligations

Andrew Walker (Pinsent Curtis Biddle)

INTRODUCTION

This chapter examines the obligations contained in the UKLA's Listing Rules applicable to companies on the Official List following the listing being obtained. It then briefly examines the differences in the obligations imposed on AiM listed companies in these areas. Finally, it discusses the potential consequences of non-compliance.

In the case of both the Official List and AiM the continuing obligations can be divided into the following categories:

- requirements to furnish information in relation to the company to the market. As the introduction to Chapter 9 of the UKLA's Listing Rules states: 'Observance of the continuing obligations is essential to the maintenance of an orderly market in securities and to ensure that all users of the market have simultaneous access to the same information';
- requirements in relation to transactions undertaken by the company, in the case of the Listing Rules, so as to give share-

holders a power of veto over the decision of the board with regard to, primarily, acquisitions and disposals above a particular size; and

- restrictions on directors and others in senior positions in the company with regard to dealing in the company's shares. This provides an additional tier of protection for shareholders and the market, over and above that given by company law and 'insider trading' legislation, against any abuse and, perhaps more importantly, the perception of abuse, by the company's directors and other senior employees.

OFFICIAL LIST

Provision of information

Basic obligation

The principal obligation with regard to the provision of information is to publicize, without delay, any significant matters that are not public knowledge and which may lead to a substantial movement, either downwards or upwards, in a company's share price. Examples of such matters could include the decision to buy or sell a significant business, the insolvency of a major customer, a major price hike by a supplier or the commencement of a challenge to a key patent.

Publication of the information must be effected through the Company Announcements Office of the London Stock Exchange (CAO). The CAO operates the 'Regulatory News Service' or RNS, which provides a mechanism for the orderly provision of company information to the market. Announcements submitted to the CAO are processed and then released to subscribers (who are mainly London Stock Exchange member firms and press agencies) via a data feed, so that those who make a market in the shares have equal access to the information as it is announced.

The obligation to notify does not arise if such matters are simply pending, or in the course of negotiation where knowledge of them is restricted to, and held in confidence by, the company's advisers and any person with whom it is negotiating (and also others who fall into certain limited categories, such as government officials and trade union representatives). The company may not supply the information to any other person until the CAO is notified; and so where, for example, a matter is to be disclosed at a shareholders' meeting or to another stock exchange (in the case of a company with a second listing overseas), arrangements must be made for simultaneous notification to the CAO.

If the company anticipates a 'leak' of its confidential information, then a 'holding announcement' must be made indicating that the company expects to release information that may lead to a share price movement.

A company can apply for a dispensation from its obligation to make disclosure of key information where disclosure would prejudice its 'legitimate interests'. However, given the propensity of information to 'leak' thus presenting an unfair advantage to those in the know, such dispensations are given only rarely.

The company is of course obliged to take all reasonable care to ensure that the information it notifies to the CAO is not misleading, false or deceptive and does not omit anything likely to affect the import of such information.

Other requirements

The Listing Rules provide further detailed requirements for the disclosure of information; the more significant of these are discussed below.

Corporate governance and directors' remuneration

This has of course been a hot area in recent years and an additional layer of regulation and indeed cost has been introduced. By way of background, as a result of the deliberations of the Cadbury and Greenbury Committees and their reports, the 'Combined Code' was prepared setting out principles of corporate governance and best practice for listed companies. Areas covered by the Code include board composition, directors' remuneration policy, relationship with shareholders and accountability and audit. The

Listing Rules provide that a company must include in its annual report and accounts, a) a narrative statement as to how it has applied the *principles* in such a way as 'enables its shareholders to evaluate how the principles have been applied', and b) a statement as to whether or not it has complied with the *provisions*, together with reasons for any non-compliance. There are also detailed requirements regarding the information to be included in the annual report with regard to directors' remuneration.

Financial information
The CAO must be notified without delay after board approval of the preliminary statement of annual results and dividends (and in any event within 120 days of the end of the period to which the statement relates). The Listing Rules also provide detailed requirements for the contents of a company's annual report and accounts. There is also a requirement to produce half-yearly results and detailed rules as to what they should contain. Clearly, this all results in additional significant cost and management time over and above that necessary for audited accounts.

Profit forecasts/estimates
The Listing Rules control what a company may say about its profits prior to audited figures being made available. In particular, any such statement must be clear and unambiguous and include a statement of principal assumptions; and, where included in Listing Particulars, a Class 1 circular (discussed below) or circular on refinancing proposals, it must be accompanied by an accountants' report.

Rights as between holders of securities
The basic principle is that shareholders in the same position must receive equality of treatment. In particular, shares must be issued on a pre-emptive basis, unless shareholders permit otherwise. (In practice, the general principles of company law will usually achieve the same result for shareholders.)

Changes in capital

A company is also obliged to notify the CAO of certain specific matters in relation to its share capital, such as any proposed change in its capital structure and changes in the ownership of its shares where notified to it pursuant to the relevant Companies Act requirements.

Information in relation to directors

Any change in directors is to be notified, as is any change in their or their connected person's ownership of shares and details of the grant and exercise of options. Directors' service contracts are to be available for inspection at the company's registered office and AGM.

REQUIREMENTS IN RELATION TO TRANSACTIONS ABOVE A CERTAIN SIZE

The Listing Rules provide for the division of transactions entered into by a listed company into certain 'classes', dependent on size, with different requirements applying for each. It should be noted that any transaction of a subsidiary undertaking of a listed company is deemed to be that of the listed company and is accordingly brought within this regime.

Transactions of a revenue nature in the ordinary course of the company's business are excluded from the requirements, as are transactions that comprise the issue of securities or other fundraising not involving the acquisition or disposal of a fixed asset.

'Class 1' transactions

Basic principles

The Articles of Association of virtually every UK company delegate to its directors the power to effect an acquisition or disposal of any subsidiary, business or other assets owned by the company; there is, in broad terms, no restriction as a matter of company law (in the absence of bad faith) on the exercise of those powers, even where this would constitute a fundamental change in the nature of the company's operations.

However, in the case of companies on the Official List, the UKLA considers that this does not give sufficient protection to shareholders. Therefore, shareholder consent is required before a transaction above a certain size, referred to as a 'Class 1' transaction, can be completed by a listed company.

In broad terms, a transaction will be 'Class 1' where the assets being acquired (or disposed of) will increase assets, profits or turnover by 25 per cent (or decrease them by this amount if the transaction is a disposal) or where the assets being acquired or disposed of have a value equal to or greater than 25 per cent of the listed company's market capitalization.

The Listing Rules provide comprehensive definitions as to precisely what is meant by 'assets', 'profits', 'consideration', etc and a detailed and careful analysis and calculation needs to be carried out by the listed company and its financial advisers to ascertain into which 'class' any transaction falls for Listing Rules purposes. Where the bald application of the class test produces an anomalous result or where the calculations are inappropriate to the sphere of activity of the company, the UKLA may disregard the calculation and may substitute other relevant indicators of size, including industry-specific tests.

'Exceptional' indemnities, etc

It should be noted that any 'exceptional' agreement or arrangement, such as an indemnity, pursuant to which a listed company agrees to meet the costs or losses of another person (whether or not contingent) will constitute a Class 1 transaction unless there is a 'cap' in the liability in an amount less than 25 per cent of the average of the company's profits for the last three financial years. Warranties and indemnities customarily given to underwriters and advisers are expressly stated to be not 'exceptional'. Clearly, the applicability of this rule in other circumstances may be open to question and therefore consultation with the UKLA may often be required.

Aggregation

An individual transaction that falls below the relevant threshold stands to be 'aggregated' with another transaction or transactions taking place over a 12-month period where they are linked, for example, by being with the same person. Again, in the case of doubt the UKLA should be consulted.

Preparation of circular

The almost invariable procedure is for the listed company proposing to undertake a Class 1 transaction to negotiate and enter into an agreement for the sale or purchase of a business or company subject to it obtaining the consent of its shareholders to complete the sale or disposal.

The directors of the listed company will then, with their advisers, prepare a circular to the shareholders containing a full description of the proposed transaction and explaining why they believe that it is in the best interests of the company. The circular will also contain certain other matters prescribed by the Listing Rules; the purpose of this additional information is to allow shareholders to make an informed decision on the advisability or otherwise of the directors' decision. This information includes details of the following matters for the listed company and in relation to the business or company being acquired or disposed of:

- material contracts (which does not include any contract that is entered into in the ordinary course of business) where required for making a properly informed assessment about the proposal;
- litigation or arbitration proceedings (whether actual, pending or threatened), which may have or have had in the recent past (covering at least the previous 12 months) a significant effect on the group's financial position;
- significant changes in the financial or trading position of the group since the last date to which audited financial statements have been published;
- confirmation of working capital being sufficient for the following 12 months (or, if such confirmation cannot be given, how it is proposed to raise such working capital);

- group prospects, comprising general information on the trend of the group's business since the end of the financial year to which the last published accounts relate, and, in particular, a) the most significant recent trends in production, sales and stocks and the state of the order book, and b) recent trends in costs and selling prices. This should also include information on the group's prospects for at least the current financial year, including any special trade factors or risks unlikely to be known or anticipated by the general public and which could materially affect the profits;
- detailed financial information prepared by the company's auditors including, for a typical acquisition where net assets of the undertaking being acquired will be consolidated, a comparative table or accountants' report and a statement of the effect of the acquisition or disposal on the earnings or assets and liabilities of the group;
- directors' interests in the company's shares and any previously unpublished details in relation to directors' service contracts (where, for example, a pay rise has been awarded since the publication of the last annual report and accounts) and any contracts entered into by the company in which the directors have a personal interest.

The circular must of course comply with the provisions of the Listing Rules that are applicable to all circulars. These include both general and specific requirements – the circular has to provide a clear and adequate explanation of its subject matter and a statement that where all shares in the company have been sold by the recipient of the circular, he or she should forward the circular to the stockbroker, etc through whom he or she sold the shares for onward transmission to the current holder.

Format of the circular

Preparation of the circular will typically commence as the negotiation of the transaction is being finalized, to allow the circular to be released to shareholders simultaneously with, or shortly after, the announcement of the conditional agreement.

The format of a typical circular for an acquisition of a business or shares would be as follows:

- front page: in bold letters, the nature of the proposed trans-action, surrounded by legal/regulatory 'boilerplate';
- inside front page: timetable of events – principally date of the EGM, last date for receipt of proxies and date for proposed completion of the transaction (after and subject to the passing of the relevant resolution);
- letter from the chairman: describing in more detail the nature of the transaction, the commercial rationale, the fact that it has the support of the board and a recommendation for shareholders to vote in favour at the proposed EGM. This will be drafted in close consultation with lawyers and financial advisers and will be subject to 'verification' by legal advisers, ie the veracity of every statement must be capable of being demonstrated;
- accounting information: typically an accountant's analysis of the financial performance of the business/company being acquired and a pro forma statement of net assets of the group going forward on the assumption that the transaction is completed;
- detailed summary of the conditional agreement with the seller/buyer;
- additional information section: a miscellaneous gathering together of the other required information, again prepared primarily by the company's legal advisers and subject to verifi-cation;
- notice of EGM and Form of Proxy: the final page of the circular will almost invariably be the formal notice constituting an EGM of the company at which a resolution to approve the transaction will be proposed. Such resolution is to be an ordinary resolution, requiring only a simple majority of votes cast for it to be passed.

The approval of the circular by the UKLA prior to its despatch is required.

As will be seen, the production of the circular is very much a collaboration between the company's directors (one of whom is usually deputed to supervise) and its financial advisers, accountants and lawyers. The contents of the circular remain, though, the responsibility of the directors and the circular will contain an acknowledgement of that responsibility by the directors.

Conclusion

Of course, in practice, it is extremely rare for shareholders to fail to approve a transaction in the face of a directors' recommendation, but the knowledge that shareholders' approval needs to be obtained is intended to (and probably does) act as an additional brake on any extravagant or high risk transaction being undertaken by the directors.

Transactions with 'related parties'

Basic principles

The Listing Rules provide certain safeguards against current or recent (within 12 months) directors of a listed company or any of its subsidiaries or substantial shareholders (holders of 10 per cent or more of the shares) or the associates of either taking advantage of their position. 'Associates' has quite a complex definition (and detailed consideration to the Rules always needs to be given) but includes family members, trustees of family trusts and companies where 30 per cent or more of votes attached to shares or a majority of the board are controlled by the related party.

Where any transaction is proposed between a listed company and a related party, the prior approval of shareholders, expressed through a simple majority of those voting in favour of a resolution proposed at an EGM, will be required following the receipt by them of a circular containing the relevant information prescribed by the Rules. The related party should not be permitted to vote at the meeting.

Exclusion of certain types of transactions

The Listing Rules exclude the following types of transactions from the requirements outlined above:

- issues of new securities;
- employees' share schemes and long-term incentive plans;
- loans on ordinary commercial terms;
- indemnity/insurance arrangements for directors;
- underwriting on normal commercial terms;
- joint investment arrangements between the company and the related party where the terms offered to the company are no less favourable than those offered to the related party;
- smaller transactions where the relevant ratios (as referred to above) are less than 0.25 per cent.

Where a transaction with a related party is of a size such that none of the percentage ratios referred to under 'Class 1 transactions' above is more than 5 per cent but one or more exceeds 0.25 per cent, there is no requirement for a circular/shareholder approval. The transaction may proceed subject only to a) the UKLA being provided with a written confirmation from an independent adviser acceptable to the UKLA that the terms of the proposed transaction are fair and reasonable so far as the shareholders of the company are concerned, and b) an undertaking being given to the UKLA to disclose full details in the company's next published accounts.

For the purpose of determining size, the UKLA can require aggregation of transactions over a 12-month period.

Contents of a related party transaction circular

The steps for the preparation of the circular are as for a Class 1 transaction. The information to be included is, however, more restricted (unless, of course, because of its size the transaction is also Class 1). The main information to be included is as follows:

- full particulars of the transaction, including the name of the related party and the nature and extent of the interest of such party in the transaction;
- a statement by the directors (other than those who are related parties or their associates or directors of a related party) that the transaction is fair and reasonable so far as the shareholders in the company are concerned and that the directors have been so

advised by an independent adviser acceptable to the UKLA. Typically this would be the company's usual financial adviser or stockbroker;

- a statement that the related party will abstain and has taken all reasonable steps to ensure that its associates will abstain from voting at the relevant EGM;
- in the case of a transaction where the related party is a director, or an associate of a director, of the company or any subsidiary, details of the following in relation to that director – his or her interests in shares in the company, his or her interest in any recent transactions entered into by the company and details of his or her service contract;
- the holders of major interests in shares in the company;
- material contracts (to the extent relevant with regard to how a shareholder should vote);
- significant changes since the end of the period to which the last audited accounts relate.

'Class 2' and 'Class 3' transactions

A transaction is 'Class 2' where the assets being acquired will increase any of the assets, profits or turnover by 5 per cent (but less than 25 per cent) or where the assets being acquired or disposed of have a value equal to or greater than 5 per cent (but less than 25 per cent) of the listed company's market capitalization. A transaction is 'Class 3' where none of the relevant percentages is 5 per cent or more.

While no shareholder approval is required for a Class 2 transaction, the company must notify the CAO without delay after the terms of a Class 2 transaction are agreed. As one might expect, the notification has to include not only key information in relation to the transaction itself – such as the name of the person from whom the company or business was acquired (or to whom it was disposed), a description of the relevant business, the price and how it is being satisfied – but also other matters that the market might wish to know as potentially having an impact on the company's share price, being as follows:

- the value of the assets that are the subject of the transaction;
- the profits attributable to those assets;
- the effect of the transaction on the listed company, including benefits expected to accrue;
- details of directors' service contracts;
- in the case of a disposal, the application of the sale proceeds and, if shares or other securities are to form part of the consideration, whether such securities are to be sold or retained.

A further notification must be made if any significant change in information provided occurs or any significant new matter arises which would have been disclosable had it arisen at the time of the preparation of the earlier notification.

No notification is required for a Class 3 transaction, save that if the company releases any details to the public, these details must also be notified to the CAO. The notification must also include basic information on the transaction, including how the consideration is being satisfied, the value of the assets acquired / disposed of and, in the case of a disposal, the effect on the company of the disposals.

Reverse takeovers

Where one of the percentage ratios referred to under 'Class 1 transactions' above is 100 per cent or more, there is clearly a fundamental change in the nature of the business or control of the company. This circumstance, referred to as a 'reverse takeover', will lead to the suspension of the company's listing pending shareholder approval and the preparation of new listing particulars.

Purchase of own securities

The Listing Rules provide detailed requirements for a company wishing to purchase its own securities, whether on or off market. These are principally concerned with notification of proposed and actual purchases.

Communications with shareholders

The Listing Rules provide that, unless a circular to shareholders is of a specified nature or complies with certain requirements, the prior approval of the UKLA is required. In practice, the bulk of circulars for which UKLA approval is sought are for Class 1 and 'related party' transaction circulars. It would be fairly rare for a listed company to want to do something other than this, the nature or manner of which would give rise to a prior UKLA approval. All circulars have to be copied to the UKLA.

Companies with particular characteristics

The Listing Rules vary or supplement the requirements in relation to the following types of company: overseas companies, property companies, mineral companies, scientific research based companies, investment companies, investment trusts, unit trusts, public sector bodies, innovative high growth companies and venture capital trusts. The details of the particular requirements for these entities are outside the scope of this book.

RESTRICTIONS ON DIRECTORS AND OTHERS DEALING IN THE COMPANY'S SHARES

The Listing Rules provide that a listed company must require its directors and any other employee/director of a subsidiary within the listed company's group to comply with the 'Model Code' set out in the Listing Rules. It should be emphasized that this requirement is in addition to the requirements of the common law (for example, the fiduciary duty of a director to act in the best interests of the company) and statute (such as the 'insider trading' legislation which criminalizes trading in listed securities in certain circumstances).

A summary of the key requirements and prohibitions contained in the Model Code is as follows. a) A director must not deal in securities of the company at any time without receiving clearance to do so from the chairman or other designated director or during 'close periods'; b) a director must not be given clearance to deal when any matter exists which constitutes unpublished price-sensitive information (whether or not the director is aware of the matter) and the dealing would take place after the time when it has become reasonably practicable that an announcement will be required, or otherwise when the chairman or designated director has reason to believe that the dealing would be in breach of the Model Code.

A 'close period' is the period of two months immediately preceding the preliminary announcement of the company's annual results or, if shorter, the period from the year end to the time of the announcement and, a) (if the company reports half-yearly) the equivalent period preceding the interim report, or b) (if the company reports on a quarterly basis) the period of one month or, if shorter, the period from the end of the quarter to the time of the announcement, preceding the quarterly report for each of the first three quarters. During a close period a director can be presumed to be in the possession of unpublished price-sensitive information regarding the forthcoming financial results.

These restrictions on dealings in the company's shares also apply to the grant or acceptance of options, to the exercise of options and to dealings in options by directors, and extend to dealings of all such types by members of the director's immediate family and connected companies and trusts. It is the duty of the director to ensure no dealings take place by such persons at times when he or she would be prohibited from dealing.

The chairman or other designated director may permit dealings in other circumstances, for example a sale of shares to meet a pressing financial commitment or an exercise of options where the final date for exercise is imminent and the director could not reasonably have been expected to exercise the option at an earlier time.

AiM

Provision of information

Basic obligation
The AiM Rules are virtually identical to the Listing Rules in their requirement for immediate disclosure of price-sensitive information to the market. In the case of companies listed on AiM, this requirement is actually given statutory force by the Traded Securities (Disclosure) Regulations; however, the enforcement of this legal requirement is delegated to the London Stock Exchange as operators of AiM, so this distinction is in practice perhaps not of great significance.

Other requirements
The AiM Rules provide for specific disclosure of information on a much more limited basis than the Listing Rules. Disclosure is, however, required of the following:

- directors' interests in shares and the grant to or exercise of options by directors (and also connected persons);
- changes in holdings of shares notified to the company pursuant to the statutory requirements (principally for those holding 3 per cent or more);
- resignation and appointment of directors;
- annual audited accounts within six months of the end of the financial period to which they relate;
- a half-yearly report within four months of the end of the period;
- any material difference between actual and any previously published estimate or forecast of financial performance;
- resignation of or other change in nominated adviser or broker.

(Certain other more minor matters are also disclosable, but are not included here.)

Rules in relation to transactions

An important difference between continuing obligations in the Listing Rules and the AiM Rules (if not the key commercial difference) is that there is no requirement for an AiM-listed company to obtain prior shareholder approval for transactions above a certain size or with related parties. Consequently, AiM-listed companies are spared the attendant delay, cost (in terms of preparation of the circular and holding of an EGM) and uncertainty of obtaining approval in these situations.

Instead, the AiM Rules provide specific requirements with regard to disclosure of the details of transactions to the market through the CAO. A brief summary of these requirements is given below.

'Substantial' transactions

A transaction is deemed to be 'substantial' if any of the ratios, as discussed above, is greater than 10 per cent.

The CAO is to be informed without delay of the details of any substantial transaction as follows:

- particulars of the transaction, including the name of any company or business being bought or sold, where this is relevant;
- a description of the business carried on by, or using, the net assets that are the subject of the transaction;
- the consideration and how it is being satisfied (including the terms of any arrangements for deferred consideration);
- the value of the net assets that are the subject of the transaction;
- the profits attributable to the net assets that are the subject of the transaction;
- the effect of the transaction on the issuer including any benefits that are expected to accrue to the issuer as a result of the transaction;
- details of any service contracts of proposed directors of the issuer;
- in the case of a disposal, the application of the sale proceeds;
- in the case of a disposal, if shares or other securities are to form part of the consideration received, a statement whether such securities are to be sold or retained; and

181

- any other information necessary to enable investors to evaluate the effect of the transaction on the issuer.

Transactions with a related party

In the case of a transaction with a related party (which in broad terms has the same definition as in the Listing Rules) where any percentage ratio (as discussed in 'Class 1 transactions' above) is 5 per cent or more, then the requirement is to disclose the same information as for a substantial transaction, plus the name of the related party and the nature and extent of its interest in the transaction. The notification must also include a statement by the directors (excluding any director who is a related party) that, in their opinion, having consulted with the company's nominated adviser, the terms of the transaction are fair and reasonable so far as shareholders are concerned.

Details of any transaction with a related party where any percentage ratio exceeds 0.25 per cent must be included in the issuer's next audited accounts.

Reverse takeovers

As with a company on the Official List, the announcement of a reverse takeover will lead to a suspension of listing. An explanatory circular must be sent to shareholders and their approval obtained before restriction of listing.

Restrictions on directors and others dealing in the company's shares

The principles are the same as for a company on the Official List and, in particular, the Model Code applies.

NON-COMPLIANCE

The first and most important point to make is that it would appear that material non-compliance with the Listing Rules is, perhaps surprisingly, pretty rare.

Clearly, the system of requiring applicants for listing to be sponsored (and therefore in effect fairly thoroughly vetted by professional organizations known to the UKLA) and the *de facto* monitoring of those companies by brokers, auditors and investors generally all help in this regard – any infringement will almost certainly come to light eventually, with the potential negative consequences for the company's business and share price and, possibly most significantly of all, the careers of those individuals involved.

However, where a breach does occur, the Listing Rules provide a range of sanctions (with the AiM Rules providing for similar sanctions):

- enforcement, by requiring the publication of information (or, in an extreme case by the UKLA publishing information itself);
- private censure;
- public censure;
- suspension of listing;
- cancellation of listing.

A censure may be of the company, or any one or more of its directors. In the case of wilful or persistent failure to comply with the Listing Rules, the Quotations Committee of the UKLA may require removal of the directors(s), failing which, the listing will be suspended or cancelled.

Matters other than public censure, suspension and cancellation of listing are dealt with by the UKLA's executives, with an appeal being possible to the Quotations Committee. Public censure, suspension and cancellation are determined by the Quotations Committee, with an appeal being possible to the Quotations Appeals Committee.

The Listing Rules indicate that the procedures for each Committee can be determined and published by the UKLA from time to time and that decisions are 'final'. However, the UKLA is of course constrained by the rules of natural justice and, indeed, the Human Rights Act and so its practices, procedures and decisions are, in theory, subject to control by the courts – although it is doubtful whether there have ever been more than a handful of cases, if indeed any, when the courts have been involved.

Despite the changing nature of the City and the greater possibilities of challenges to regulations such as the UKLA under the Human Rights Act, it seems unlikely, given the adverse negative publicity for the companies and individuals involved that could arise, that there will be a significantly greater role for the courts.

17

Best practice in corporate governance

Colin Aaronson (Grant Thornton)

SUMMARY

- The continued success of the City of London as a financial market depends on investors' trust in the integrity of its people and its institutions.
- Investors in companies whose shares are quoted on the London Stock Exchange need to feel confident that their interests are aligned with those of their managers, and that neither managers nor majority shareholders can abuse their position of authority to the detriment of smaller shareholders.
- Corporate governance is about the management of the company, as distinct from the management of the business. It deals with the establishment of principles and procedures to protect the interests of shareholders and to align the interests of all stakeholders in a business.

- Company law provides all shareholders with certain rights and protections. These are supplemented by the rules of the Financial Services Authority, the UK Listing Authority and AiM, and by the City Code on Takeovers and Mergers.
- The Combined Code published by the Financial Services Authority sets principles of good governance and a code of best practice.
- Part of the Combined Code is interpreted by the guidance on internal control developed by the working party led by Nigel Turnbull ('the Turnbull Committee').
- Representatives of institutional investors, such as the Association of British Insurers and the National Association of Pension Funds, have established guidelines for implementation of the Combined Code in areas such as share options, profit sharing schemes and non-executive directors.
- Company law, the Listing Rules and appended guidelines, and developing practice together constitute 'best practice in corporate governance'. Non-executive directors (NEDs) are a key element of best practice.

INTRODUCTION

Good practice in corporate governance is fundamental to the way a business is run and essential to the continued success of equity markets. Management has a duty to safeguard the assets of a business, and to act in the best interests of shareholders. Where management fails to safeguard the company's assets, particularly when they have continued to derive significant personal benefit from the business, the reputation of the market as a whole will suffer.

Corporate governance deals primarily with two issues: the management of the company and the risks associated with it; and the balancing of the interests of the stakeholders in a business. In particular remuneration policy should benefit both management and shareholders. Corporate governance is a developing area, and has attracted considerable interest following the failures of major companies such as Enron and Marconi. The role of NEDs has become the focus of particular attention, such that in 2002 the government appointed Derek Higgs to lead an independent review of their role and effectiveness.

This chapter refers throughout to the Combined Code and best practice. The Combined Code is appended to the Listing Rules, although it is not formally part of them. The Code combines the recommendations of the Cadbury, Greenbury and Hampel Committees on corporate governance. Companies seeking admission to the Full List must state whether they comply with the Code, or explain those provisions of the Code where they do not comply.

The Code is not strictly applicable to companies whose shares are traded on AiM or OFEX. However, directors will always be encouraged to embrace good corporate governance, and many of the ideas in this chapter will be applicable to AiM and OFEX companies.

In addition, representatives of institutional investors such as the National Association of Pension Funds (NAPF) and the Association of British Insurers (ABI) have issued guidance on certain aspects of corporate governance, as have the other organizations including the Department of Trade and Industry (DTI) and the investment house Hermes. The Quoted Companies Alliance has issued guidance for applying the principles of the Combined Code to smaller quoted companies (SQCs).

Management of the company

Management needs to ensure that appropriate systems of control exist to enable them to manage the business. However, the maintenance of an appropriate system of internal controls is a formal requirement for listed companies, and has been incorporated into the Combined Code.

Directors of any company, public or private, have a statutory duty to safeguard the assets of the group, and for taking reasonable steps for the prevention and detection of fraud and other irregularities. The Combined Code takes this further and states (Principle D2) that: 'The board should maintain a sound system of internal control to safeguard shareholders' investment and the company's assets.' The system of internal control should include financial, operational and compliance controls, and risk management.

The system of internal control should be tailored to individual companies. One of the ways a listed company can set itself apart from its competitors is to make clear, specific disclosure of those controls in the report on corporate governance. The Code has two provisions in this connection: a) it provides that the directors should review, at least annually, all systems of internal controls, and report to shareholders that they have done so, and b) companies that do not have an internal audit function should review the need for one from time to time.

The Turnbull Committee was convened to prepare a report giving guidance to directors on how to implement these two provisions of the Combined Code. The result was practical guidance designed to ensure that the board is aware of the significant risks faced by their company and the procedures in place to manage them. The main recommendations of the Turnbull Committee are:

- A company's system of internal control has a key role in the management of risks that are significant to the fulfilment of its business objectives. The company's internal control system should be embedded within its operations and not be treated as a separate exercise, and be able to respond to changing risks within and outside the company.
- The Turnbull guidance focuses on *significant* risks: those risks that have been identified by senior management as being potentially damaging to the achievement of the company's objectives. The company must identify risks that could undermine the reliability of internal and external reporting, the safeguarding of assets from inappropriate use, loss and fraud, and liabilities being identified and managed properly.
- Early warning mechanisms need to be established. These are reporting processes that enable the board and senior management to be alerted before a problem becomes a disaster, and at a stage when action can be taken to mitigate or overcome the situation. Key Risk Indicators should be identified and

implemented in order to give early indication of potential problems so that corrective action may be taken promptly.

Each company will face a different set of risks and will need to establish a different set of controls. Detailed guidance on the implementation of Turnbull is available from the Institute of Chartered Accountants in England & Wales on its Website.

The management of risk is one aspect of corporate governance. The other principal aspect is the establishment of a set of guidelines to ensure that where conflicts of interest arise, they are not allowed to adversely affect the interests of shareholders.

Balancing the interests of stakeholders in a business

The separation of ownership and management in a company gives rise to a potential conflict of interest between shareholders and managers. These conflicts can occur whether or not management are shareholders in a business, and can occur between majority and minority shareholders.

The Combined Code addresses these issues by establishing principles that deal with matters such as the composition of the board of directors and the procedure for setting directors' remuneration, as well as relations with shareholders, accountability and audit.

THE COMBINED CODE – COMPOSITION OF THE BOARD

The Code sets out the basic principles that govern the composition and conduct of the board. These principles are:

- A listed company should be headed by an effective board that leads and controls the company. The point is that the *board* should run the company, not individual directors, or groups of directors.
- There should be a division of responsibilities at the head of the company, to ensure no one individual or group of individuals

has unfettered powers. The chairman manages the board, the chief executive manages the business on behalf of the board. The chairman and chief executive should not be the same person, and the chairman often is not an executive. The only circumstance in which it is acceptable to combine the two roles is if the company is not trading or is actively seeking one or the other of the roles in a period of change.

- There should be a balance of executive and non-executive directors. The Combined Code states that non-executives should make up at least one-third of the board. Many companies actually have more non-executives than executives. The principle is that no one individual or group dominates decision making, and in order to do so there should be enough non-executives of sufficient calibre for their views to carry weight.

- The board should receive sufficient information in a timely manner to enable it to fulfil its duties. In simple terms this means that agendas, board minutes, reviews of internal controls and accounts are circulated in good time.

  The company secretary is responsible to the chairman and the board, and his or her responsibilities include organizing board meetings and providing information to be discussed at those meetings. The board should discuss key issues relating to the running of the business, and should have a schedule of matters reserved for its decision. The board will only be able to debate the issues properly if directors have been provided with sufficient appropriate information in time for them to prepare for the meeting itself. A good company secretary will be aware of the key issues and will be able to prepare a genuinely useful board pack. In this respect, a good company secretary is invaluable.

- Unless the board is small, a nomination committee should make recommendations on appointments, and the committee itself should be comprised mainly of non-executives. The method of board appointment should be open and transparent, and not under the control of the executives. All directors should stand down and submit themselves for re-election regularly, and at least every three years.

Non-executive directors (NEDs)

NEDs are often experienced public company directors who know and understand City rules and practice. Although their role is to ensure that the company is governed properly as a public company, they can bring considerable extra value if they have had experience in another company in the same sector. Non-executives are therefore generally older than the executives. By virtue of their knowledge, experience and personality, they should be able to stand up to the toughest and most persuasive colleague.

The majority of non-executives should be 'independent of management and free from any relationship which could affect their independent judgement'. A substantial shareholder is sometimes given the right to have a non-executive director appointed to the board to represent his or her interests. Such a director may be non-executive, but that person is clearly not independent.

The Combined Code does not define 'independence' in this context, although representatives of institutional shareholders such as the ABI and the NAPF, the investment house Hermes, and the DTI have each developed guidance on its meaning. Indicators that a NED might not be independent include service for a period exceeding 10 years; significant shareholding; previous employment within the group in an executive capacity; or acting as the nominee of a related party.

The function of NEDs is to guide and to exercise a degree of control over the executive directors. Their remuneration is designed to reflect their contribution without affecting their independence. The package will typically comprise the following:

- A modest fee to compensate them for the time spent on the company's affairs. The fee should be at a level which recognizes the value they bring, but not so high that they feel dependent on it or lose objectivity.
- A grant of shares or encouragement to buy shares in the company; this is intended to align their interest with those of other shareholders and demonstrate commitment to the business.

- Bonuses and performance-related pay are not generally thought to be appropriate for NEDs.

The role of NEDs during a flotation

The flotation process will involve a considerable amount of work for NEDs, although the board as a whole takes full responsibility for the admission document. Executives usually welcome the advice and guidance a non-executive can offer.

For companies seeking flotation, strong non-executives bring something even more valuable – the credibility that comes from their endorsing the business and agreeing to become part of it. Without good non-executives, a flotation may simply not be possible.

It is helpful if the non-executives join the board as long as possible before flotation so that they have a chance to get to know the company well, and do not delay the completion of the prospectus.

The future role of NEDs

It is true that there are limitations to the role of non-executives, but they can play an important part in encouraging good corporate governance. They should also have enough time to properly discharge their responsibilities. NEDs are increasingly being urged to limit their work commitments and concentrate on fewer director-ships.

The influence of non-executives is expected to increase in the current financial reporting climate. According to a recent survey, two out of three board directors of the top 500 companies in the UK said the influence of NEDs would increase, especially in the technology and financial services sectors.

Provided the company complies with the Combined Code and adheres to these principles, properly qualified NEDs should have sufficient influence to ensure that there are adequate checks on the conduct of the executive directors. However, there are two areas of responsibility that are so important to good corporate governance that they are devolved to sub-committees of the board. These areas are remuneration of the executive directors, and accounting and auditing.

The remuneration committee

A potential area of conflict exists between directors and share-holders when directors have the ability to determine their own pay and benefits. Accordingly, the Combined Code recommends that executive directors do not have that right, and gives the responsibility for setting directors' pay and conditions to the remuneration committee. The remuneration committee should be made up exclusively of independent non-executive directors, whose job is to determine the appropriate level of remuneration for directors, and an appropriate mix of salary, bonus and other benefits, including share options.

In order to align the interests of management with that of share-holders, pay and bonuses should be set at a level which attracts, motivates and retains staff of the right calibre, but not more than is necessary. A significant proportion of the directors' remuneration package should be performance related. Performance targets should relate to both personal performance and corporate performance. Targets should be specific, measurable, challenging yet attainable, and they should be agreed in advance. Developing practice is for shareholders to have the opportunity to vote on remuneration policy in a general meeting. Remuneration policies are then implemented on behalf of the shareholders. Proposed policy changes and actual remuneration are explained by the remuneration committee in the annual report.

Remuneration of executive directors – share options

The granting of share options is a possible source of conflict between the interests of shareholders and directors. On the other hand, a carefully constructed share option or performance-related bonus scheme can align the interests of both management and shareholders, to the benefit of both.

The remuneration committee has the responsibility for determining the terms of directors' share option schemes. Share options schemes should be arranged to reward managers who deliver strong corporate performance in the long term. Directors should be encouraged to retain shares for a period after exercise. Options should be both granted and exercised in phases, rather than all at once, and shareholders should have the right to approve all executive share option schemes.

The ABI has issued guidelines as to what its members believe constitutes an acceptable level of share options. The ABI represents the major investing institutions in the UK, and adherence to its guidelines may well be a precondition for investment by some of those institutions. The guidelines state that a company's share option scheme should satisfy the following general criteria:

- no more than 10 per cent of the number of shares in issue should be under option;
- no more than 5 per cent of the number of shares in issue should be as part of an executive scheme for directors and senior employees;
- the life of the option should not exceed 10 years, and options should not be exercisable within three years of the date of grant;
- if there are to be performance criteria, they should be selected by the remuneration committee, and should reflect significant and sustained improvement in financial performance. The performance criteria should not be capable of manipulation through a change in accounting policy.

There is some flexibility – it is usually more acceptable for a small company to issue options above those limits than a large one – but institutions will judge each case on its merits.

The audit committee

Principle D3 of the Combined Code states:

> The board should establish formal and transparent arrangements for considering how they should apply the financial reporting and internal control principles, and for maintaining an appropriate relationship with the company's auditors.

The Combined Code allocates the responsibility of appointing auditors and setting their remuneration to the audit committee. The audit committee is normally charged with considering the independence of the external audit. For example, a perceived threat to independence of the auditor is that fees for non-audit services are larger than fees for the statutory audit. In reviewing the independence of the auditor, the audit committee will consider the nature of the work undertaken, and may if appropriate request 'Chinese Walls' on the part of the audit firm.

Audit firms work within a number of guidelines issued by their institutes that are designed to protect auditors' independence, and the perception of their independence. These guidelines relate to firms as a whole, to offices of the firm, and to individual partners.

If the group has an internal audit function, the scope of the internal audit work, resources applied and independence of the internal audit team will fall within the remit of the audit committee.

The audit committee is also the forum in which auditors can raise matters that they consider to be of importance, or which give them cause for concern. Although the finance director is not a member of the audit committee, he or she may attend these meetings by invitation of the committee.

COMMUNICATING WITH SHAREHOLDERS AND THE MARKET

A company is obliged to supply the market with a certain amount of information that is set out in the Companies Act and in the Listing Rules and AiM Rules, such as annual and interim accounts. Beyond that, a quoted company must also ensure that the market is aware of all price-sensitive information – information that would, if known, affect the market's perception of a company's value and would cause a significant movement in the company's share price. If important information has not been made available to the market and investors and shareholders are basing their decisions on false or incomplete information, it is said that there is a 'disorderly market' in the shares.

A quoted company must also ensure that no group of shareholders or potential investors are in possession of information that has not been released to the market as a whole, and have an unfair advantage when trading in its shares. This is an important consideration when brokers place shares as part of second and subsequent fundraisings after the company has floated.

The company advises the market by releasing announcements through a regulatory news service. Some directors like to use announcements released in this way to 'generate interest' in their company. Setting aside the directors' reasons for wanting to make a particular announcement, it is sometimes unclear whether a piece of information actually is price-sensitive. In such cases, directors will need to consult the company's financial advisers, although where there is doubt, it is usually better to announce than not to do so.

The tone of an announcement can affect the way in which the market reacts to it. Being independent of management, and in general free from the pressure to meet market expectations, non-executives are in a good position to judge whether the tone of the announcement is appropriate in the circumstances. This is particularly relevant for Full List companies that do not have a nominated adviser to guide them.

Some types of information that are deemed to be price-sensitive in any circumstances must be released without delay. These include, *inter alia*:

- appointments and resignations of directors;
- directors' share dealings;
- changes to the holdings of significant shareholders; and
- profit warnings.

The Financial Services and Markets Act 2000 contains provisions that prohibit 'market abuse' (creating a false impression of a share's value) and gives the Financial Services Authority power to levy unlimited penalties on individuals found guilty of this offence. A company and its advisers must act responsibly, and should not therefore release an announcement until they are satisfied that it is accurate in all material respects and not misleading in any way at all.

Directors' share dealings

Directors have access to a considerable amount of confidential information, and are able to assess the effect of releasing that information on the company's share price. They are therefore in a position to profit at the expense of outside shareholders. However, directors do buy and sell their company's shares (they may need to buy shares to have any stake at all in the company, to take part in Save As You Earn schemes, or simply because they believe in the long-term prospects of the company), and sometimes they may need to sell for personal reasons. As a result, a set of rules has been developed to ensure directors can trade while minimizing the disadvantage to outside shareholders.

There is an overriding obligation not to deal on price-sensitive information, supplemented by rules to try to ensure a level playing field:

- directors cannot deal during a 'close period', which is roughly speaking the two-month period before the announcement of the company's interim or final results;
- the deal must be announced to the market without delay;
- the director should obtain permission to deal from the chairman.

Additional fundraisings and share issues

Companies go back to the market for second and subsequent fundraisings; after all, that is why most companies float in the first place. This will usually be in the form of a placing by the broker with a number of institutional investors. The company can do so if its Articles of Association allow it to issue the required amount of new shares. Shareholders must also have given the directors authority to issue shares without having to offer them to existing shareholders first. Section 89 of the Companies Act gives existing shareholders pre-emption rights – the right of first refusal – over any new shares issued. Section 95 of the Act gives shareholders the right to disapply these pre-emption rights, and to allow directors to issue shares other than to existing shareholders.

It is clearly in shareholders' interests for the directors to have some flexibility. However, placings dilute existing shareholders' interest in the company, and limits need to be set. The ABI guidelines suggest that directors should not be able to place for cash more than 5 per cent of the number of shares in issue. For smaller companies the percentage figure can be higher, but what constitutes an acceptable level is a matter of judgement and one that the company's non-executives and advisers will decide.

In practice shares have to be placed at a discount to the market price (otherwise the institutions could buy in the market). The more liquid the stock and the smaller the placing relative to the market capitalization of the company, the smaller the discount needs to be for the placing to be a success. The Listing Rules state that shares cannot be placed at a discount of more than 10 per cent of the mid-market price, unless the UKLA is satisfied that the company is in severe financial difficulties, or there are other exceptional circumstances. AiM companies are not subject to such constraints, but before placing the shares they should consult with their nomad to agree an appropriate placing price. If institutions will only invest at significantly below the market price, it suggests that the market price does not take account of facts known to the potential placees, and that there may in fact be a disorderly market in the shares.

CONCLUSION

Best practice in corporate governance is essential to protect the interests of all shareholders and to align the interests of shareholders and management. Not all best practice provisions will be appropriate to every company, particularly smaller ones – they must be tailored to the company's size and circumstances. It is a developing area and the development of the non-executive role is likely to be particularly interesting.

18

Best practice in corporate communications

Peter Binns (Binns & Co)

The key to success in being a publicly listed company lies in coming up to expectations on the profit front – repeatedly and consistently. Meet the forecasts of your broker and everything else should fall into place.

There are four financial calendar events (or six should quarterly results be produced) that matter: the announcement of your interim and final trading results, the publication of your annual report and accounts and your Annual General Meeting. A company needs to manage expectations ahead of and after results, but it should also aim to meet the key opinion formers on a regular basis during the year – outside of the close periods, which are 60 days ahead of the announcement of figures. At the least, such meetings should be timed to coincide with the release of the interim and final results and following major transactions or significant fundraising exercises.

After going public, any serious quoted company needs to consider how it will achieve proper value and reach its institutional investors. Therefore, by priority, the target audiences are: the fund managers, broker analysts, the press, retail investors and the market makers. Each influences the others to different degrees.

Timing is also key. Every company is competing for attention in a crowded marketplace. Hundreds of announcements are issued daily, thousands weekly. The likes of fund managers, analysts and the press are courted by all. The bigger the company, and therefore the bigger the story, the more attention it will receive. It is no good putting your head above the parapet just once a year and then complaining about 'the lack of understanding' in the marketplace.

Good PR needs to be planned and well timed. Failure to get the message heard will affect perceptions. This in turn can lead to difficulties in raising capital or securing an acquisition. Investor interest and loyalty must be nurtured. A long-term, coordinated corporate and financial communications programme, with clearly defined goals, is a vital part of that process.

There is no doubt that many companies are neglected in their attempts to develop through organic or acquisitive activity because their corporate message is often misdirected and poorly constructed.

GETTING TO KNOW YOU

Managing expectations is therefore paramount to a successful PR campaign. To ensure accuracy and consistency in the message you want to deliver, it is essential that the PR team develop an intimate knowledge of your operations and strategy from the beginning. They should familiarize themselves with your products and services, liaise with your senior management and identify potential issues. At the same time, they will ascertain how your business is perceived by your target audiences, via market research among established contacts in the general marketplace, in the investment community and media.

A good PR firm can then help to address any misconceptions, fill in the gaps in knowledge and build a strong and accurate profile of your business and its aspirations. The objective will be to provide your business with a clear identity – one that stresses its unique qualities and potential – while helping to handle the sensitive and controversial issues that every business faces from time to time. The process should include a review of your Web site, corporate literature and other promotional material, together with advice on presenting to investment audiences and dealing with the media.

It is best to have two senior executives deployed on an account. They should be supported by IR, media and research specialists and an experienced secretarial team. Regular strategy planning and review meetings must also be initiated from the outset of working together and an 'open line' established between the account team and your executives.

As a quoted company, the best results are achieved by running a media and investor relations campaign in tandem.

NEWS AND ISSUES MANAGEMENT

A news flow should be outlined and during the course of a year your company will be involved in a series of price-sensitive issues. Announcements will need to be made to the Stock Exchange. It is essential that all public statements are handled sensitively. A good PR firm will be experienced in drafting, editing and distributing announcements of this kind, using both the official channels of communication and its own long-standing contacts. It will be used to meeting deadlines, performing under pressure and delivering results. First announcements are issued on the Stock Exchange at 7 am, while trading in London begins at 8 am. The London stock market closes at 4:30 pm; last announcements are issued at 6:30 pm. All announcements may be sent by embargo if desired.

MEDIA RELATIONS

Building strong and productive relationships with leading opinion formers in business and financial circles is a key ingredient of any communication programme. Leading consultancies have developed a mutual trust with some senior journalists, which enables them to open doors that might otherwise remain closed. This includes London based foreign correspondents, access to whom provides a valuable international dimension, and local, regional and trade press to provide employee and commercial benefits.

The Internet's speed, reach and interactivity have also created new opportunities for dialogue and relationships with stake-holders.

DIRECT LINK TO THE LONDON STOCK EXCHANGE

A direct link to the London Stock Exchange is vital. At Binns & Co, as at other leading financial PR firms, an accredited computer link to the Stock Exchange for releasing statutory and press information on RNS enables the firm to transmit company announcements, however long and complex, to the Exchange at whatever time of day or night they are agreed. Because the link is direct there are no security concerns.

Releases need to be factual, accurate and adhere to the City codes of practice and Stock Exchange rules governing the content of announcements. They must also be approved by a company's financial advisers.

Financial news flow embraces any announcements that are deemed price-sensitive. They include:

- financial calendar events;
- trading updates;
- mergers and acquisitions;
- fundraisings;
- disposals;
- institutional or notifiable share stakes, director shareholdings or interests;
- comment on share price movements in excess of 10 per cent of the current price;
- board and senior management changes and appointments;

- product launches, innovations and developments;
- strategic alliances;
- change of auditors;
- drilling reports;
- net asset value(s);
- purchase of own securities;
- buy back of own shares;
- litigation;
- capital expenditure;
- licensing agreements;
- joint ventures;
- other corporate developments.

FINANCIAL CALENDAR

As a Stock Exchange listed company, your communications programme will inevitably revolve around your financial calendar. Attention to detail is imperative. Timing is essential to achieve maximum impact – an issue on which your PR firm should advise. It should also draft and distribute statements and arrange meetings with the relevant target audiences.

MERGERS, ACQUISITIONS, DE-MERGERS, TRANSACTIONS

Every leading PR firm works closely with the City's leading M&A specialists, whether it be on high profile bid battles or smaller bolt-on acquisitions, and should be able to slot in quickly and effectively to become a key member of an advisory team.

CRISIS MANAGEMENT

Even in the best-run companies unexpected problems occur. What distinguishes the better companies from the rest is the manner in which a crisis is handled. The key is to prevent long-term damage to the company's credibility. Experienced public relations advice can be crucial. Leading PR firms operate around the clock to ensure that expert counselling is just a phone call away.

BUSINESS, TRADE AND TECHNICAL

The specialist press plays an important role in shaping opinion among customers and competitors, sector analysts, potential investors and the national media. Any top PR adviser has a network of contacts in the trade and technical media with whom to liaise on particular stories and ideas. They should receive all price-sensitive announcements. Coverage can be generated in appropriate special surveys and via exclusive stories. At leading PR firms, a team of specialist consultants and writers is also retained to meet requests for briefings, feature articles, symposium papers and marketing documents.

INVESTOR RELATIONS

It is recognized that communicating with shareholders is essential to companies if they seek to get across the right message and increase their profile within the City and regional investment communities. Any company should present itself regularly to a wide audience of investment professionals. One of the main objectives of a PR/IR firm is to continue to expand a client's contacts and effect introductions and meetings.

Above all, a successful investor relations programme should seek to build a knowledgeable and supportive following among institutional and retail investors and brokers. This will help maintain the company's rating within its peer group and facilitate future corporate activity.

The programme should be proactive. It must be executed with care, complying with legal requirements and Stock Exchange regulations. It must be coordinated with the activities of the company's stockbroker and other corporate advisers.

With the growth of shareholder democracy, there is a demand among investors for rapid and accurate information on a wider range of companies. This demand is also reflected in the growth of Web sites devoted to market news.

DATABASE, SHARE PROFILE

A leading financial PR firm will maintain an extensive database of sector, mid-cap and smaller company analysts, and London and regional-based private client brokers, enabling the assembly of a target audience tailor-made to each individual client. The database needs regular updating as the City job market can, at times, resemble a merry-go-round.

A share register and profile of the leading institutional fund management groups, together with their relevant funds, should be updated, on a quarterly basis, by the company registrar, company secretary, stockbroker and financial PR adviser.

ANALYSIS OF SENTIMENT

A good PR firm can also interpret City analysts' views on a company, to help manage expectations and report to management and the Board by:

- preparing regular reports;
- monitoring progress of forecasts and recommendations;
- summarizing analysts' views on clients and their peers.

INVESTMENT MARKET RESEARCH

There will be many outside influences on your company's share price of which you are unaware. This is why your PR adviser will recommend an approach that begins with a detailed survey of attitudes among broker analysts, market makers and institutional and private investors. It is vital to know at any one time who your share-holders are and the range of their expectations. Bear in mind, too, that institutions will not necessarily have a single opinion. Individual fund managers within one organization often have conflicting views of different objectives: one may be a buyer, another a seller. Companies need to understand who holds their shares within an institution, and why. Remember also that the continuing change in the shareholder base makes it imperative that potential new shareholders are actively cultivated. Fund managers also change jobs, but not as frequently as brokers.

Before embarking upon an investor relations programme, it is vital to ascertain:

- the criteria on which investors will measure the company's performance;
- investors' perception of trading results and other announce-ments;
- the identity of the best informed and most influential commen-tators;
- the principal sources of news information and comment;
- the degree of satisfaction with the delivery of the communica-tions programme;
- the availability of senior management to meet investors;
- what demand there is for meeting line management or visiting operations;
- investors' views on management, finances and corporate gover-nance.

In addition:

- What is your present reputation and how do you want to be perceived?
- Are there past, current and future issues that might impact on the profile?
- Is there a sufficient following in the marketplace from flotation, subject to the company's size and stock availability?

A well-rounded PR programme should thus embrace briefings, one-to-one presentations, road shows, shareholder analysis, and a continuous, sensible news flow.

MARKET OPINION RESEARCH

Aside from investment community feedback, to audit the effectiveness of your communications strategy – either on a regular or occasional basis – PR firms may conduct detailed attitude surveys of the total audience, such as legislators, journalists, customers, employees or any other constituency of interested parties.

RESULTS BRIEFINGS

Briefings for analysts and meetings with the press on the day a company announces its interim or final results form a part of most investor relations programmes. Interest is subject to a company's size, track record and growth potential.

Follow-up calls should be made to obtain feedback from those who attend, and sentiment reports produced after events. Channels of communication should be monitored, including the changing status of analysts or commentators, in order to ensure that your message reaches its target audiences quickly and efficiently.

BROKER/INVESTOR COMPANY VISITS

Analysts and investors often find site visits useful in expanding their understanding of a company's operations – but not in the hectic results season of March and September. While they offer the opportunity to meet and talk to line management, and build confidence in the underlying strength of your operational team, they also provide another occasion to deliver your key messages at some length and without distraction. Typically, events such as plant openings, new acquisitions, the launch of new products and follow-ups to results or trading statements, provide an ideal motive for such a visit. A PR/IR firm will advise on timing, draw up a recommended guest list, and take care of arrangements, both for domestic and overseas visits. Again, feedback will be gathered after meetings.

REGULAR MEETINGS

The rules concerning what you may say on these occasions are tightly drawn. The PR firm will be able to brief and advise as required, and sit in on the meetings.

ROAD SHOWS

A road show allows you to take your story to the local investment community rather than wait for them to come to you. It may be prompted by a fundraising or some form of M&A activity, but it should be undertaken with longer-term goals in mind. Leading financial PR advisers will have extensive experience in organizing successful, cost-effective UK road shows in the City and major centres throughout the UK, as well as overseas in capital centres in Europe, the United States, Australia and elsewhere.

INVESTOR SHOWS

Sponsored shows in the City held by leading corporate finance and securities houses, and the nationwide exhibitions organized by the likes of the Guild of Private Shareholders, or by the media, are also worthwhile platforms in helping get across the appropriate messages to the investment community. It should be part of the PR firm's job to advise you on their merits, timing, likely attendees, theme and content.

SPECIALIST INVESTOR SEMINARS

Leading financial PR firms are experienced in the inception, promotion and organization of their own investor seminars that have been co-sponsored by City institutions. At Binns & Co, for example, seminars have focused on the oil and gas and alternative energy sectors.

Participation as a speaker at one of these seminars has proved an excellent avenue for a company to establish itself as an authority in its sector or on a specific issue affecting that sector. A varied and topical agenda with good quality speakers can draw a valuable City audience comprising institutional investors, stockbroker analysts and the press.

OTHER SERVICES

A PR firm can offer other services, including:

- writing, production and design of literature, especially the annual report and accounts;
- slides and flipcharts;
- corporate video production.

Any PR consultancy should be given a clear understanding of the limits of its brief and when there is a need to go to a higher authority. Be sure to conduct regular and honest reviews of progress and achievements to ensure the relationship continues to flourish.

SUMMARY

Financial and corporate PR can and should add value. There are two rules, above all, to bear in mind. First, agree what constitutes success from the programme and benchmark the results constantly against the targets. Remember too, that financial PR must adhere to rules and regulations. Second, accept that success or failure belongs to the whole advisory team and that PR cannot be expected to deliver unaided.

Services should be cost-effective, based on management, executive and administrative time and charged either hourly, by project or on an annual retainer. They should be built upon research, forward planning, performance and getting the right results by offering a proven, reliable and effective service.

Here's a list of what good PR brings to the party:

- close, long-standing relationships;
- an ability to interface at all levels;
- a track record;
- market management;
- an established network of contacts;
- placing power;
- a proactive approach;
- a reactive approach subject to story conditions;
- research-driven campaigns;
- streetwise advice;
- an ability to deliver.

19

Reviewing the company's pension plan

Richard Harwood (Grant Thornton)

INTRODUCTION

The provision of pension arrangements for employees does not vary significantly between different types of employer. A public company, private company, partnership or sole trader may well still operate the same type of pension arrangement for their staff. Similarly, the legislation affecting pension provision applies equally to all types of employer.

Differences in the nature of pension provision lie more in the areas of what is practical for the employer concerned. Generally speaking, a public company will have a larger number of employees and more diverse operations. It is these factors that are likely to affect the choice of pension provision for such a company.

Upon going public, the major change is the ownership of the company. Typically, companies before flotation are owner-managed by a small number of individuals working closely together. They are often well known to each other, or even family. For these people, the company represents both an investment of their own personal wealth as well as their employment. Pension provision is a combination of long-term funding for retirement income and of withdrawing wealth from the company in a tax-efficient manner.

After going public, the owners and directors are, largely, separated. Therefore, the owner-manager effect is significantly weakened and pension provision ceases to be a holistic financial planning exercise, moving more towards funding for employees' retirement.

LEGAL RESPONSIBILITIES OF THE EMPLOYER

There was no obligation on employers to provide access to pension provision until the Welfare Reform and Pensions Act 1999 came into force in April 2001. This Act applies equally to all employers, regardless of their status. The general requirement of the Act is that all employers with more than five employees are obliged to provide access to pension provision for the bulk of those employees. There are exemptions in the case of certain employees who can be excluded on the basis of age, or if they earn below the National Insurance lower earnings limit.

The Act compels an employer to provide access to pension provision; however, it is not necessary for this to be funded by the employer. As a minimum, an employer must provide access to a Stakeholder Pension Scheme allowing employees to make their own contributions into a low-cost money purchase pension arrangement. The decision whether or not an employer wishes to fund pension provision is still based upon his or her own business requirements.

TRENDS IN OCCUPATIONAL PENSION PROVISION

The more traditional way for an employer to provide a group pension arrangement has been in the form of a defined benefit scheme. With this type of scheme, a fund exists to provide an income to members after retirement, based upon a formula relating to earnings and service. An actuary calculates the required contribution by the employer to sustain the fund. As the fund value fluctuates, it may be in surplus or deficit when compared to the amount required to provide the underlying benefits.

The employer contracts to fund the defined benefit scheme. Future required contributions can, therefore, reduce (or premium holidays can be taken) when fund performance is high, but significant additional contributions may be required where fund performance is insufficient, causing the scheme to fall into deficit.

Many large older plcs operate pension schemes on a defined benefit basis. This is more as a result of the age of those employers than their present situation. As benefits that have been previously promised must be provided, many companies are concerned about possible deficits within their funds and the resultant increase in required contribution. Therefore, there is a growing trend for companies to move their provision away from defined benefit schemes towards defined contribution schemes and there are very few new defined benefit schemes now being established.

A defined contribution scheme is less complex to administer and involves a known cost to the employer. The principle is that an employer makes contributions of a pre-determined amount, usually calculated on the basis of a percentage of earnings. These monies are invested into individual earmarked funds, which are ultimately used to provide retirement benefits for the members. Growth in the fund and the variations in future annuity rates merely affect the value of the ultimate benefits for the member rather than the cost to the employer. As these involve a fixed cost, they are more palatable for many employers. They are not, however, necessarily as well received by the employees as they do not offer a pre-determined level of pension and the level of members' benefits are not established until retirement is reached.

Due to the nature of legislation it has become common for employers to operate a Group Personal Pension Plan. This involves the individual members establishing their own personal pension plan and the employer making contributions to it. In terms of the overall funding, these schemes behave in a similar way to an occupational money purchase scheme. As previously indicated, the choice of scheme is largely dependent upon an employer's specific situation.

When a company is going public, the shareholders are far less likely to be directly related to the company and members of the scheme. Therefore, they are less likely to appreciate the benefits of a defined benefit scheme and more likely to consider it as a potential liability for the future.

FRS17

The Accounting Standards Board issued rules concerning the valuation of scheme assets and liabilities set out in *FRS17 Retirement Benefits,* which came into effect in 2001. These mean that the funding level of pension benefits must be disclosed in a company's accounts and are fully effective for accounting periods ending on or after 22 June 2003, with disclosures required for accounting periods ending on or after 22 June 2001. The principle is that, for defined benefit schemes:

- scheme assets are measured at a fair value;
- scheme liabilities are measured at an approximation of fair value using the projected unit method;
- liabilities are discounted at the current rate by a high quality corporate bond of equivalent term and currency to the liabilities;
- the resulting net asset or liability is presented separately on the balance sheet after other net assets.

This has the effect of disclosing to the public the assets and liabilities of a defined benefit scheme.

In a situation where the company is going public the tendency is for external investors to seek to ensure the best possible return on their purchase. As such, the FRS17 regulations could result in a disclosure of a potential debt on the employer that could have a major effect on their willingness to invest and on the flotation. Similarly, there are a number of occasions where the company balance sheet is likely to be examined and any disclosures in relation to a pension scheme deficit are likely to prove detrimental. As such, the required disclosures are likely to have a more significant effect on the business activities of a plc than on an owner-managed company.

Already, the requirements of the FRS17 regulations are stated as the reason for a number of major plcs moving their pension provision from a defined benefit to defined contribution basis.

SMALL SELF-ADMINISTERED SCHEMES

Over the past three decades, there has been a growth in Small Self-administered Schemes (SSAS). They are occupational pension schemes specifically developed for owner-managers.

The basis of an SSAS is that there is one fund to provide benefits for the individual members, usually on a money purchase basis. However, the funds are 'notionally earmarked'. This means that they are not segregated for each individual member but the calculation of contributions and benefits does make an assumption in relation to the allocation to individual members. The funds can be invested as one entity and the scheme allows investments in the company, in the form of share ownership or loans to the employer.

It is also very common for SSAS schemes to purchase commercial property which would then be free from tax on any capital gain. The property is often occupied by the company itself, so the SSAS is used to make a purchase that the company may otherwise make itself.

These types of arrangements are particularly used by entrepreneurs who are looking to make high levels of pension contributions due to their tax efficiency, but who would rather have control over the investments and, preferably, use the funds in relation to the company.

This type of arrangement is, therefore, particularly used by owner-managers or where the directors of a company are close family or friends. In the case of flotation, there is often an influx of directors who have little or no stake in the company and who are, therefore, less willing to invest pension monies within the company. As a result, there is less benefit from running this type of arrangement and fewer directors are willing to do so. Such a scheme can continue to operate or, where there are a number of new directors joining the fund who do not wish to participate, contributions can cease, but the existing benefits can remain held within the arrangement.

HIGH EARNERS

The 1989 Budget introduced a salary cap for the calculation of pension benefits. This was originally introduced at a level of £60,000 per annum and has been increased subsequently in an attempt to keep pace with inflation. The salary cap for the 2002/03 tax year stands at £97,200 per annum.

The effect of the salary cap is that it fixes a ceiling for the calculation of maximum pension benefits. An approved pension scheme cannot be used to provide benefits for earnings in excess of the relevant cap. Where membership of the scheme began before the cap was introduced, the relevant member can continue to have benefits provided based upon his or her full earnings.

Given this situation, it is quite possible that incoming directors to a company that has recently gone public could have earnings above the cap and reduced pension benefits in relation to their entire earnings. For this reason, Funded Unapproved Retirement Benefit Schemes (FURBS) were developed. These are pension arrangements for individuals' earnings above the cap but which do not have all of the tax benefits of an approved arrangement. It is common for such schemes to be established alongside an approved occupational pension scheme.

As these schemes are not approved, there are a number of differences, the key one being that contributions are taxed as a benefit-in-kind for the employee. It is, therefore, common for the employer not only to make the contribution but also to fund the additional tax liability. Although relatively expensive, this does mean that equivalent benefits can be provided to equalize benefits for different key employees. It is more likely that a plc would have the funds and inclination for this type of funding.

20

Transactions by quoted companies

Colin Aaronson (Grant Thornton)

SUMMARY

- Companies often float to enable them to grow through acquiring companies by issuing shares.
- Depending on the size of the transaction and whether the company is on AiM or the Full List, the company may either have to announce the details of the transaction or seek shareholder consent.
- There are rules to protect shareholders where there is a change of ownership or control of the company.

INTRODUCTION

When a company comes to the market, it must describe the nature of its business in some detail in its prospectus, and it must also identify the major shareholders. On the basis of that information the UKLA and AiM admit companies, and investors buy shares in them.

If the nature of the company changes fundamentally, for example by selling its existing business and acquiring a different one, the UKLA and AiM will cancel the company's listing and require the company to reapply for admission.

A transaction that fundamentally changes the nature of a business is referred to as a 'reverse transaction'. Not all transactions change the nature of the business but they all alter it to some degree. Depending on the size of the transaction relative to the size of the company, the company may have to announce the details of the transaction, or even obtain shareholder consent.

The Listing Rules and the AiM Rules are concerned with the nature of the business. The question of change of control and the protection of shareholders is dealt with separately by the 'City Code on Takeovers and Mergers' ('the City Code' or 'the Code') and is regulated by the Panel on Takeovers and Mergers ('the Panel'). The UKLA, the Exchange and the Panel all enforce these rules rigidly to ensure that investors' interests are protected and safe-guarded, as part of a concerted effort to protect the reputation of London's financial markets and ensure that they remain pre-eminent.

THE CLASS TESTS

Whenever a quoted company undertakes a transaction outside of its ordinary operations, such as a substantial purchase, a sale of assets, or the acquisition or disposal of a business, it must perform a set of five tests, which are specified in the AiM Rules and Listing Rules. These tests, which are known as the 'class tests', measure the impact of the transaction on the company.

In simple terms, the five tests compare the following measures for both the quoted company and the asset or business being acquired, based on the latest publicly available information:

- consideration for the asset being acquired or sold, compared to the market capitalization of the company;
- turnover;
- profit;
- gross assets;
- gross capital (consideration or market capitalization plus shares not being acquired, long-term debt and net current liabilities).

The relevant figure for the asset or business being bought or sold is divided by the equivalent figure for the quoted company, to give a number expressed as a percentage. The class tests produce a set of percentage figures, and on the basis of the highest of those percentages, the company is obliged to carry out the actions shown in Table 20.1.

Sometimes the class tests give anomalous results, such as when an investment company acquires a business with a larger turnover than itself. In such circumstances, the UKLA and the AiM teams have authority to disregard such a result or request that a substitute test is applied to assess the size and impact of the transaction.

Sometimes it is unclear whether a transaction is outside a company's ordinary operations for the purposes of these rules; the disposal of a factory or other property, for example, is a transaction that sometimes falls into this grey area. The company, through its advisers, may have to negotiate this point with the UKLA or the Exchange.

Related party transactions

When a company enters into a transaction with a related party, it must perform the class tests as are required for substantial transactions. If the class tests result in a figure greater than 5 per cent for an AiM company, or 0.25 per cent for a Full List company, it must comply with additional rules designed to protect independent shareholders. In general, a related party is either a director or a substantial shareholder, or a person connected with them (eg, children, spouses).

Table 20.1 *The class tests for quoted company transactions*

Percentage	Full List	AiM
Less than 5%	'Class 3' transaction requiring release, through a regulatory news service, of basic information about the transaction	Not applicable
5 – 25%	'Class 2' transaction requiring release, through a regulatory news service, of more detailed information about the transaction	Not applicable, but see 10% transaction size below
Greater than 10%	See Class 2 transaction above	Announce details of transaction via a regulatory news service. Contents are largely the same as for a 'Class 2' transaction by a Full List company
Greater than 25%	'Class 1' transaction requiring circular to shareholders, giving details of transaction. Shareholders must approve the transaction. Similar information to 'Class 2' must be released through a regulatory news service	Not applicable
100%	Reverse transaction, requiring the approval of shareholders in an EGM and a new application for admission	Reverse transaction, requiring the approval of shareholders in an EGM and a new application for admission

If, for example, an individual were to buy an asset from a quoted company of which he or she is a managing director, the managing director would be treated as a related party and the acquisition would constitute a related party transaction. In a situation such as this, there is a possibility that the deal might be priced to the benefit of the managing director and to the detriment of other shareholders.

The related party rules seek to protect the independent shareholders by ensuring that certain information is disclosed and that, in certain circumstances, shareholders have the right to approve or reject a transaction. On the basis of the class tests, it must take the action shown in Table 20.2.

Where the company and its advisers are unsure whether the related party rules apply to a transaction, they should consult with the UKLA or the Exchange.

The class tests make it difficult for Full List companies to enter into sizeable transactions without having to revert to shareholders

Table 20.2 *The class tests for related party transactions of quoted companies*

Percentage	Full List	AiM
0.25%	Advise UKLA of the proposed transaction, provide written confirmation from an independent adviser acceptable to the UKLA that the transaction is fair and reasonable as far as the shareholders of the company are concerned, and undertake to include details of the transaction in the next published annual accounts	Not applicable
5%	Same information as 'Class 2' transaction, along with information about the related party and its interest in the transaction, requiring release through a regulatory news service. A circular must be sent to shareholders, whose approval of the transaction must be obtained	Announce details of transaction via a regulatory news service. It must provide details of the related party and the transaction, and a statement that the independent directors, having consulted with the company's nominated adviser, believe that the transaction is in the best interests of shareholders. Shareholders do not specifically need to give approval

for approval. On AiM the rules are much less restrictive, which is a reason companies might seek to transfer from the Full List to AiM. It is also a reason why AiM may be a more suitable market for acquisitive companies.

THE PANEL ON TAKEOVERS AND MERGERS

The Panel is not specifically interested in what the company does, but is concerned with changes to the individuals and groups that control it.

The Panel has no status in law; rather it is an organization that derives its authority from the esteem in which it is held throughout the City. It is located in the Stock Exchange building, has a small permanent staff, but is mainly staffed by capable and well trained professionals on secondment from investment banks and brokers, accountancy firms and firms of solicitors. It has no sanctions other than to criticize and, in extreme cases, to 'cold-shoulder'. This has hardly ever happened, as the practical consequences of cold-shouldering are too serious for a company to contemplate.

The rules of the Panel, known as the 'City Code' or 'Takeover Code' (or the 'Blue Book', from its cover), represent a shared set of values and beliefs as to what constitutes fair and reasonable behaviour, distilled from years of practice by a community of financial professionals. The City Code applies to all UK public companies, whether quoted or unquoted (as well as some private companies), of which the centre of management and control is in the UK. When such a company becomes subject to a possible change of control, the Panel must be consulted and the Code applied.

The percentage shareholding that gives control will differ from company to company: 20 per cent of a FTSE-100 company may give a shareholder effective control, whereas 40 per cent of a much smaller company may not. An arbitrary limit must be established and the City Code regards 30 per cent as giving control.

THE CONDUCT OF TAKEOVERS

Depending on the proportion of shares in public hands, going public exposes a company to the possibility of an unsolicited takeover bid. An acquisition-minded company might also try to buy another quoted company. Whether an approach is friendly or hostile, the way in which such companies must conduct themselves is set out in the Takeover Code.

The Code sets out 10 general principles that should guide all parties involved in public company takeovers, and which find their practical application in the 38 rules of the Code. The basic principles by which a company should conduct itself are:

- Treat all shareholders equally and fairly:
    - the offeror must treat all shareholders similarly;
    - information must not be made available to some shareholders that is not available to all;
    - the oppression of minority shareholders is wholly unacceptable.
- Companies must act responsibly:
    - an offer should only be announced after the most careful consideration;
    - a person or company making an offer may only do so if he or she has the resources to implement such an offer;
    - shareholders must be given sufficient information to make an informed decision;
    - information sent to shareholders must be prepared with the highest level of accuracy and care;
    - parties to an offer must ensure that a false market in the offeree company's shares does not exist.
- Directors must act with integrity:
    - when advising shareholders, directors involved in an offer must not have regard for personal or family shareholdings;
    - any action that the directors of an offeree company take that might affect the outcome of an offer must be approved by shareholders in a general meeting.

The detailed rules are set out in the Blue Book and are available on the Takeover Panel's Web site (www.thetakeoverpanel.org.uk). A company that is the subject of an approach will be guided by a suitably qualified adviser. However, there are a number of rules that are relevant in most, if not all, takeover situations.

Rule 1

The offer must be made to the board of a company, or its advisers (who will inform the board). The point is that the offer must be made to the board, via its chairman or advisers, and not to a major shareholder or the managing director.

The board has the right to know who is making the offer (if the offer is being made by an adviser), and to be satisfied that the offeror has the resources to carry out the offer.

Rule 2

Secrecy is paramount and advisers will, as a matter of course, advise their clients of the need for discretion at the outset. However, announcements must be made in certain conditions:

- when a firm and unconditional offer is made to the board;
- when a Rule 9 obligation is incurred (see below);
- when, following an approach (but not a firm offer), the company is the subject of speculation or rumour and there is an untoward movement in its share price;
- when negotiations are to be extended to more than a very restricted number of people.

Responsibility for announcements in these circumstances lies with the offeree company, although there are circumstances before an offer is made where the potential offeror may be obliged to make an announcement.

Rule 3

The board of the offeree company must obtain competent independent advice, and make the content of that advice known to shareholders.

Rule 9

A shareholder who acquires shares such that he or she holds more than 30 per cent of a company, or who already has more than 30 per cent and acquires any more shares at all, is required to make an offer to all other shareholders to buy his or her shares.

There are exceptions to this rule, of which the most important to growing companies is probably the dispensation from Rule 9 known as the 'whitewash'. A quoted company may buy another, possibly larger company, and pay for it with shares. The vendors of the company being acquired will become shareholders in the acquiring company. If the company being acquired has few shareholders, those shareholders either alone or 'in concert' might come to hold more than 30 per cent of the acquiring company. Under Rule 9, they would normally be required to make an offer to all other shareholders.

If this rule were applied in such circumstances, most acquisitions using paper as consideration would simply not take place. There is therefore an exemption to Rule 9 whereby shareholders in the acquiring company must be sent a document giving details of the company or asset being acquired, and information about the new controlling shareholders and their interest in the company. Those shareholders must approve the transaction at an EGM, at which they must specifically agree that the Rule 9 obligation should not apply to those new controlling shareholders. Those new shareholders are the party being 'whitewashed'.

When a whitewash happens in the context of a reverse takeover, the whitewash document forms part of an AiM admission document or Listing Particulars.

Rule 11

A cash offer is required when an offeror has acquired more than 10 per cent of a company from a date 12 months before the offer was made. The offer must be at the highest price paid by the offeror during that 12-month period and thereafter.

21

Enhanced financial reporting requirements

Nick Jeffrey and Ruth Cooke (Grant Thornton)

INTRODUCTION

This chapter looks at the effect of 'going public' on your financial reporting requirements. You will need to think about your annual report, which now becomes far more than a set of accounts. You will also need to think about other reporting requirements such as 'interim reports' and 'preliminary announcements'. The relationship with your auditor will not change in essence, but the work undertaken by the auditor and interaction with the auditor during the course of the year will change. The final section of this chapter looks at future developments: the financial reporting environment is changing all the time, and we discuss some of the major changes on the horizon for listed companies.

Your financial information will have a far higher profile

'Going public' means just that – everything you do and say is subject to far more scrutiny than you will have been used to. This includes the annual report. The annual report, including the financial statements, is subject to far more public scrutiny than the reports of companies that are not listed. This scrutiny comes from two directions. Analysts, institutional investors, private investors and potential investors use the annual report to confirm or otherwise the market interpretation of other (unaudited) information in the public arena. Quite apart from those interested in your results, other parties are interested in the more detailed disclosures in the annual report. The Financial Services Authority (via the UK Listing Authority), the Financial Reporting Review Panel, and the DTI are all capable of enforcing changes to your accounts, which would result in potential public censure.

The higher profile of your annual report has its benefits. Wider readership means that the annual report could, and should, be used as a selling document. Throughout this chapter, we will give you some ideas for promoting your company and for setting yourself apart from your competitors.

Is your accounts department up to the job?

Before you think about specific details of the changes you will encounter on becoming a listed company, you need to think about your accounting function. The Listing Rules require a listed company to produce more information in a speedier timescale than a private company, whilst retaining accuracy. In addition, the results themselves are under a great deal of scrutiny. This obviously places pressure on the accounting function. Handy hints here are to practise faster reporting before becoming a listed company, and put in place a sound, credible accounting function with sufficient resources before the company applies for a listing.

THE ANNUAL REPORT OF A LISTED COMPANY

What doesn't change?

The directors have certain responsibilities regardless of whether the company is listed or not. Preparation of the annual report is still the responsibility of the board of directors. The financial statements taken as a whole must still give a true and fair view of the state of affairs of the group and the company and of the results of the group for the year. The financial statements still have to be properly prepared in accordance with the Companies Act 1985.

In preparing those financial statements, the directors are still required to:

- select suitable accounting policies and then apply them consistently;
- make judgements and estimates that are reasonable and prudent;
- make certain statements with regard to applicable accounting standards;
- make statements regarding the going concern of the entity.

AiM, OFEX companies

The Listing Rules, and the requirement to comply with the Combined Code, do not apply to companies listed on AiM or OFEX. This is part of the attraction for smaller quoted companies (SQCs) that do not wish to be part of the more rigorous regulations and rules applied to companies on the Full List.

However, good practice is an excellent way of setting yourself apart from your competitors, which may not take their public status as seriously. In particular, the following sections on 'Your annual report is a selling document', and 'Internal controls', when applied specifically to your business, can make a difference.

The Listing Rules – additional financial reporting requirements

Chapter 12 of the Listing Rules sets out 'continuing obligations relating to matters of a financial nature'. These apply to fully listed companies only.

Sections 12.41–12.42 deal with the annual report, of which the main points are:

- The annual report must be published as soon as possible after the accounts have been approved, and in any event within six months of the year end (AiM six months; OFEX five months).
- Directors' interests in 'contracts of significance' should be disclosed; that is, contracts entered into by the company from which a director stands to benefit. Disclosure should include the nature of the contract and the amounts and terms involved.
- The directors must make a statement that the company is a going concern. They must also state any supporting assumptions or qualifications if there is any possible doubt about the company's ability to continue as a going concern. This is an explicit confirmation by the directors – private companies only need to make disclosures where there is doubt about the going concern assumption.

Your annual report is a selling document

Typically, your annual report will include reviews from the chairman, the chief executive and the finance director. There will still be a directors' report on behalf of the entire board, and in addition there will be a corporate governance report and a report on remuneration. A notice of the AGM is usually attached.

When briefing investors and the press, it is sound advice to 'under-promise and over-deliver'. The key elements to communicate are that you have strong management in tune with the industry and with the business, and that you are driving the business forward while controlling the associated risks.

Corporate governance

Corporate governance is an often-used phrase. For the purposes of this book, it is taken to relate to those principles addressed by the Combined Code – see Chapter 17.

Section 12.43A of the Listing Rules requires the directors to give a statement of compliance with the Combined Code throughout the period. In the event of non-compliance for part of that period, the directors should state the code provision not complied with, reasons for non-compliance and steps the board intends to take to address the issue.

The directors are also required to say how the board has applied the principles of the Combined Code, 'providing explanation which enables its shareholders to evaluate how the principles have been applied'. Typically, the disclosures address relations with shareholders, how the board operates, accountability and audit and internal controls (see below).

Creative use of the 'Investor relations' section of the company Website should be advertised.

Internal controls

The Combined Code requires that directors disclose the significant financial, risk management, operational and compliance controls. Many SQCs restrict themselves to (familiar) internal financial controls. These reports could be far more useful if they set out significant other controls.

Without taking risks, a business will wither away and die. That is not to say that taking risks to drive the business forward cannot be mitigated, and you should use the annual report to tell everyone about your high quality risk management procedures. The directors should disclose policies specific to their business and say how those policies have been applied and improved during the year. For example, a utilities company might discuss environmental issues; an owner of nightclubs might discuss relations with the local community, local authorities and the police; a company that is heavily dependent on IT in its business might talk about disaster recovery.

Directors' remuneration

Section 12.43A requires the board to report to shareholders on directors' remuneration. Required disclosures include information on share options and elements of remuneration, policy on granting of options, details of defined benefit schemes and details of pension contributions.

Section B of the Combined Code requires disclosure of the remuneration policy and details of the remuneration of each director. Remuneration policies are generally delegated to the remuneration committee, which should be made up of non-executive directors (NEDs), all of whom should be independent within the meaning of the Combined Code.

The better annual reports disclose specific (ie numerical) targets for allotment of share options and payment of performance-related bonuses. The DTI would like the directors to produce graphs comparing performance of the company with comparator companies. Representative associations of institutional investors are increasingly raising questions on directors' remuneration at Annual General Meetings. The more progressive companies ask the members in AGMs to approve the remuneration policies.

Other narratives written by the directors for the annual report

The Operating and Financial Review (OFR) is coming. The concept of an OFR has been around for some time, and has been discussed in separate consultations by such parties as the DTI (under the Company Law Review), the ASB and, internationally, by the IASB.

The OFR will replace the directors' report for listed companies, and will incorporate many aspects of developing good practice in areas such as SEE reporting and risk management analysis.

SEE reporting

Social, Environmental and Ethical (SEE) Reporting, or Corporate Social Responsibility (CSR) Reporting, is a developing area that is generally seen as an extension of good corporate governance.

Common subjects are recycling and energy conservation. The higher quality annual reports set measurable targets and obtain assurance from the auditors on numerical disclosures. A company with significant business interests in the Third World might discuss its interaction with the communities where it is based and where it works, discuss employment and employee welfare policies, and talk about relationships with local government.

FRS 13 – Derivatives and other financial instruments

The standard contains requirements for numerical disclosures linked with the mix of fixed and floating interest rates, instruments held in foreign currencies, and maturity of financial liabilities. The standard also requires the directors to identify risks arising from the company's financial instruments, state the policies to mitigate those risks, and disclose how those policies have been applied during the year. There should also be a general discussion of the entity's activity, structure and financing.

FRS 14 – Earnings per Share (EPS)

EPS is a number much loved by analysts. In the past it has been open to 'creativity', and so the ASB issued a standard to make every listed company's EPS disclosures comparable.

Basic EPS is calculated using the earnings attributable to ordinary shareholders divided by the weighted average number of shares in issue during the year. An additional EPS figure must be given where there are dilutive potential ordinary shares and dilutive options (ie, EPS would fall if the potential shares were issued). Additional EPS figures may be given. Reconciliations of all EPS figures to basic EPS should be given in a table.

OTHER REPORTING REQUIREMENTS

Interim report

Section 12.46 of the Listing Rules states that a company must present a half-yearly report as soon as possible, and in any event within 90 days of the period end (AiM and OFEX – within three months of the period end). The Listing Rules have some required content including an explanatory statement. Good practice is set out in guidance from the ASB, which recommends the inclusion of the primary statements, significant notes, and comparatives.

There is no requirement for the interim report to be audited, but if an auditor reviews the statement and then reports to the board, the review report must be published alongside the interim accounts.

OFEX requires that results are published quarterly during the first three years that a company is listed on OFEX and where there is a fundamental uncertainty or going concern statement in the audit report.

Preliminary announcement

Section 12.40 of the Listing Rules states that a company must notify a Regulatory Information Service of its preliminary statement of annual results and dividends without delay after board approval, and in any event within 120 days of the period end.

This should include paid and proposed dividends and at least the items required for interim reports in a format consistent with the annual report. The announcement must include the audit report if it is qualified. Additional 'good practice' guidance is given by the ASB. In essence the guidance recommends that the primary statements (profit and loss account, balance sheet, cash-flow statement and statement of recognized gains and losses) and significant notes are given, and this has now become a generally accepted practice.

The Listing Rules require that the preliminary announcement must be agreed by the company's auditors prior to release. When combined with the requirement of board approval, this means that the audit must be complete, that issues arising from the audit have been resolved, and that the annual report is essentially complete subject to minor disclosures and typographical errors.

AiM and OFEX have no requirement to make a preliminary announcement, but in the event that the broker advises one should be made, good practice would follow the requirements of the Listings Rules.

RELATIONSHIP WITH YOUR AUDITOR

What doesn't change

An audit is an audit. Your auditor still has to give an opinion as to whether the financial statements give a true and fair view, and whether they have been prepared in accordance with the Companies Act 1985. The auditor will still need to collect sufficient evidence to support that opinion, and the auditor will still discuss the results of the audit with the directors.

The annual report

You are likely to find that you will have more discussions with your auditor on the annual report as a listed company than you were used to as a non-listed company. In part this is due to there being more rules for a listed company, but there is also an expectation on the part of the reader that the annual report will contain far more information for a listed company. When giving advice, your auditor will talk about 'best practice'. Best practice develops over time, and reflects the changing market expectations and the financial reporting environment.

A company following best practice demonstrates to the market that it takes its reporting responsibilities seriously. Best practice for SQCs is often a watered down version of best practice, applied to its own business and appropriate to a company of its size. Your auditor will be steering you away from policies that are considered to push the boundaries of acceptable practice; in this regard it is no different to the advice for a private company. The difference is that the advice for a listed company carries even more weight.

A large part of the advice that you will receive will not necessarily relate to the numbers in the annual report but will relate to disclosures. The point here is that investors do not like surprises. If an unexpected message has surprised the market, it is very difficult to regain lost goodwill. Full disclosure should help to avoid such surprises.

The Combined Code

Only certain parts of the statement on application of the Combined Code must be reviewed by auditors to reflect the Company's compliance and the auditors will report if it does not: The seven Code provisions are:

- A1.2 Schedule of matters reserved for the board.
- A1.3 Procedure agreed by the board for directors in the furtherance of their duties to take independent professional advice if necessary.
- A6.1 NEDs appointed for specific terms.
- A6.2 Re-election of directors at least every three years.
- D1.1 Directors explain responsibility for preparing the accounts.
- D1.2 Board to present a balanced and understandable assessment of the company's position and prospects.
- D3.1 Audit committee of at least three directors, all NEDs, the majority of whom are independent. Committee to have written terms of reference.

In addition, elements relating to remuneration of the directors are within the scope of the audit report.

Accounting assistance from your auditor

Auditors are not permitted to prepare the accounts of listed company clients, except in an emergency. Provision of this service by the auditor would constitute a breach of the ICAEW's guidance on the independence of auditors. However, the auditor will need to ensure that the company has systems capable of producing information of a sufficiently reliable nature on a timely basis.

FUTURE DEVELOPMENTS

International Financial Reporting Standards (IFRS)

On 7 June 2002, the European Council of Ministers gave final approval to the Regulation requiring the use of IFRS in the consolidated accounts of companies governed by the law of an EU Member State whose securities are admitted to trading on a regulated market of any Member State at their balance sheet date. The regulation comes into force for accounting periods beginning on or after 1 January 2005.

In the UK, the Regulation will apply principally to the group accounts of companies with a full Stock Exchange or AiM listing. The DTI will consult on whether the UK should exercise the option to extend the Regulation, for example to individual quoted company accounts.

The company will need to give comparatives that are IFRS compliant; that is, for accounting periods ending on or after 1 January 2004. The opening position in the 2004 accounts will need to be IFRS compliant; that is the accounting period beginning on or after 1 January 2003. So, in this context, 2005 is really 2003!

Company Law Review

The Steering Group of the Company Law Review made its recommendations to the DTI for improvements to Company Law in Spring 2002. The DTI will implement those proposals on a piecemeal basis over the coming years.

22

Realizing value from the listing and tax implications of listed shares

Robert Langston (Grant Thornton)

REALIZING VALUE FROM THE LISTING

Altering the number of shares in issue prior to the listing

The company will usually need to increase the number of shares in issue prior to the float to ensure that the existing shareholders' holdings are not massively diluted once the public issue is made – and this will be done either via a bonus issue or a partition. A bonus issue involving all the shares in the company does not increase (or reduce) the value of the shareholders' holdings, and no tax liabilities will normally arise. Equally, a partition simply subdivides one current share into a greater number of shares with the same total nominal value.

If, however, some of the existing shareholders have the value of their holdings increased, and others reduced, a 'tax-free benefit' may be obtained. In these circumstances, it is advisable to seek clearance from the Inland Revenue that liabilities do not arise under the anti-avoidance provisions of s703 ICTA 1988 (transactions in securities). There may also be implications under the value shifting provisions. Provided that the restructuring is undertaken for commercial (rather than tax avoidance reasons), no such liability should arise.

Cash and loan notes

Although it is relatively unusual for shareholders in private companies to directly realize full value during the listing process, it may be possible to do so. Typical methods used – and the tax implications of each – are shown in Table 22.1.

If any of these methods are used, they must be used only with the knowledge and acquiescence of the nominated adviser (or sponsor), and must be fully disclosed in the prospectus.

Enterprise Investment Scheme

For new investors (or existing shareholders wishing to purchase additional shares from the public offering), the Enterprise Investment Scheme (EIS) offers two tax reliefs for the purchase of shares.

EIS income tax relief

Investments of up to £150,000 in EIS qualifying shares will reduce the investors' personal income tax liability by 20 per cent of the qualifying investment.

If the investment is made prior to 5 October, up to half of the investment can (at the investor's option) be treated as made in the previous tax year. This may be advantageous if the investor does not have a tax liability in the year of investment that is sufficient to fully utilize the EIS income tax relief.

Table 22.1 *Typical methods used and the tax implications of each*

Selling shares on the market to supplement the new issue	Capital gains tax (CGT) will be charged on any gain, subject to any reliefs that may be available. CGT is charged at a taxpayer's marginal (highest) rate of tax, which in many cases will be 40%. The vendors are likely to be required to pay for the stamp duty liability (0.5% of the consideration) that applies to the acquisition of these pre-existing shares.
Payment of a dividend	For higher rate taxpayers, income tax will be charged at an effective rate of 25% on the net amount of the dividend.
Issue of loan notes or cash on restructuring	As part of pre-float restructuring, share holdings can be reorganized or exchanged into new companies (see above); if cash is also paid as part of the exchange, a gain may arise which is chargeable to CGT. By using appropriate loan notes rather than cash, this tax charge may be reduced and/or deferred. However, under certain circumstances this realizing value from the reconstruction may increase the danger of a tax charge under s703 ICTA 1988 (see above).

EIS capital gains tax relief

If investors have made capital gains (during the tax year in which they invest) from three years before until one year after, the amount of any gain may be reduced by the amount invested in EIS qualifying shares. There is no restriction on the amount of relief that may be available.

The relief is a deferral only, and the gain will be charged to tax on a subsequent disposal of the EIS shares.

Qualifying conditions

For both EIS income tax relief and EIS capital gains tax relief, shares are qualifying shares if they satisfy a number of conditions, the most important of which are:

- the shares must be *issued*, rather than purchased;
- the company must be an 'unquoted' company (see below for the definition of 'quoted' for tax purposes);
- the gross assets of the company must not exceed £15 million prior to the issue and £16 million immediately after issue;
- the company must carry on a qualifying trade.

For EIS income tax relief, the following conditions must also be satisfied:

- the investor must not be 'connected' with the company (or its subsidiaries) during the period beginning two years before the issue of shares and ending three years after; an individual is connected with a company if he or she:
  - is an employee
  - is a director receiving more than a commercial rate of remuneration, or
  - holds more than 30 per cent of the shares.

Share options issued pre- or post-float

There are many reasons why a company may decide to implement a share scheme:

- to remunerate employees in a tax efficient way;
- to incentivize employees to perform better;
- to attract and retain staff;
- to enable employees to participate in the ownership of the company.

Schemes may be made available to all employees or can be targeted at selected groups of employees only. Share schemes are either approved by the Inland Revenue or unapproved. Those that are approved are in general less flexible, but offer favourable tax breaks. The most common types of employee share schemes are:

- unapproved share option schemes;
- Company Share Option Plans (CSOPs);

- savings-related schemes (SAYE or Sharesave);
- Share Incentive Plans (SIPs);
- Enterprise Management Incentives (EMI).

A company may decide to implement a share scheme as part of its planning prior to floating in order to tie in the management team, as the options can be designed to lapse if the team leaves prior to a certain date, and take advantage of low market value and therefore a low exercise price under approved schemes.

Shares options issued following the float will have a more immediate value to employees as they will have a market on which to sell them (but there may be tax consequences of such options for the company – see below).

Loans to purchase shares

If investors take out a qualifying loan to purchase shares, they may be entitled to tax relief on any interest paid, at their marginal rate. Although there are a number of conditions that must be satisfied, qualifying loans include loans to acquire shares in a close company, ie a company that is controlled by five or fewer shareholders, or any number of shareholders who are also directors, and which is an unquoted trading company (although relief is not available if EIS income tax relief has been claimed). Qualifying loans also include loans to acquire shares in a company that is controlled by employees, but ignoring those employees holding 10 per cent or more of the shares and which is an unquoted trading company. (See below for the definition of 'quoted' for tax purposes.)

THE TAX IMPLICATIONS OF LISTED SHARES

What is a 'quoted' share for tax purposes?

The operation of many tax provisions is dependent on whether shares in a company are 'listed' or 'quoted' on a 'recognized stock exchange', or 'readily convertible assets' – ie a market exists for trading.

For tax purposes, these definitions do not have their normal meaning. Fully listed shares count as 'listed' or 'quoted' on a 'recognized stock exchange', but shares listed on AiM or OFEX do not. Shortly after the AiM was opened, the Inland Revenue confirmed in a press release (20 February 1995) that:

> There are a large number of references in tax legislation to securities that are listed or quoted on the Stock Exchange or other recognized stock exchanges. As the Financial Secretary's speech makes clear, securities on AiM will not fall to be treated as quoted or listed for tax purposes. They will therefore qualify for the various tax reliefs available for unquoted securities.

Similar assurances were made in respect of OFEX-listed shares.

However, listing on any exchange is usually sufficient to create a trading market for shares, and therefore they will be 'readily convertible assets' whether listed on AiM, OFEX or the Stock Exchange.

Individual Savings Accounts (ISAs)

ISAs replaced Tax Exempt Special Savings Accounts (TESSAs) and Personal Equity Plans (PEPs) as the government's tax-free incentive to save money. There are broadly two types of ISA. First, there is a *maxi ISA*, which can have up to three components – equity, cash and insurance. There is a subscription limit of £7,000 on the equity component, or £3,000 if the cash and/or insurance components are also used. Secondly, there is a *mini ISA*, which has only one of the three components, with a subscription limit of £3,000 if equity or cash, and £1,000 if insurance.

Income arising on investments in an ISA is free from income tax, and the disposal of any shares held in the equity component is free from capital gains tax (CGT). Only quoted shares can be held in either a maxi or a mini ISA.

Loss relief

Ordinarily, capital losses (ie, where an asset is sold for less than it was purchased) are not available to set against income. However, s574 ICTA 1988 allows relief against income for capital losses on *unquoted* shares. This will typically have the effect of reducing a vendor's tax liability for the year in which shares are sold.

A further point to note is that in order to qualify for this relief, shares must be 'subscribed for' rather than purchased from another shareholder (whether on the market or otherwise).

Capital Gains Tax (CGT) hold over relief

A gift of shares (and indeed all assets) is treated for tax purposes as an ordinary sale. Where a gift takes place to a 'connected person' (broadly, family members) this sale is deemed for tax purposes to take place at market value, and it is possible that a taxable gain could arise. s165 TCGA 1992 therefore allows any gain arising on a gift of business assets to be 'held over' – ie deferred – until the *transferee* disposes of the shares. Any tax liability is therefore also deferred.

Hold over relief is also available on sales at below market value to connected persons. In order for this hold over relief to be available, shares must be shares in a trading company (or group) *and* be either unquoted, *or* shares in the donor's 'personal company', ie the transferor holds 5 per cent or more of the voting rights.

Capital Gains Tax (CGT) taper relief

For individuals, taper relief replaced indexation allowance in 1998 as the method of giving relief for inflationary rises in the value of shares. The amount of relief available depends upon the length of time for which shares have been held, and whether during that time those shares are 'business assets' or 'non-business assets' (or both).

For periods prior to 6 April 2000, shares are business assets if the company is a trading company (or group) and the shareholder holds 25 per cent or more of the voting rights, or the company is a trading company (or group) and the shareholder is a full-time employee who holds 5 per cent or more of the voting rights.

For periods after 5 April 2000, shares are business assets if:

- the company is an *unquoted* trading company (or group); or
- the company is a trading company (or group) and the shareholder is a full-time employee; or
- the company is a trading company (or group) and the shareholder holds 5 per cent or more of the voting rights; or
- the company is a non-trading company (or group) and the shareholder is a full-time employee who holds 10 per cent or less of the issued shares.

Venture Capital Trusts (VCTs)

VCTs are investment funds that provide a number of tax benefits:

- dividends from VCTs are free from income tax;
- gains on disposal of shares in VCTs are free from capital gains tax (CGT);
- income tax relief is available at a rate of 20 per cent on investments of up to £100,000 into VCTs;
- CGT can be deferred on other capital gains of up to £100,000.

In order to qualify as a VCT, an investment fund must meet a number of conditions, most importantly that 'qualifying holdings' must make up at least 70 per cent of the investment portfolio. Qualifying holdings are shares in unquoted companies, which were *issued* to the VCT (rather than purchased on the market).

If a company ceases to be an unquoted company (for instance it progresses from AiM to a full listing), its shares are deemed to meet the qualifying holding test for a further five years. VCTs may therefore be a good source of investment for a listing on AiM or OFEX.

Enterprise Investment Scheme (EIS)

In order to qualify for income tax and capital gains tax relief under the Enterprise Investment Scheme, shares must be unquoted at the time of issue and there must exist no arrangements for them to become quoted. Relief is not, however, withdrawn if unquoted shares later become quoted (for instance if relief has been given in respect of shares issued on entry to AiM and the company subsequently acquires a full listing).

Inheritance Tax (IHT)

Shares that are 'business property' for inheritance tax purposes may qualify for business property relief (BPR), which removes some or all of their value from the taxable estate on death. Shares are 'business property' if they are:

- unquoted; or
- quoted and the shareholder controls the company; and
- the company's activities do not wholly or mainly consist of the holding of investments, dealing in land shares or securities.

Unquoted shares attract BPR at 100 per cent, removing their full value from the estate. Qualifying quoted shares attract relief at 50 per cent, removing half of their value from the estate. If the company holds any non-trading assets, relief may be restricted.

A summary is presented in Table 22.2.

Share options granted to employees

Share options granted to employees under a scheme that has not been approved by the Inland Revenue (see above) are usually chargeable to both tax and National Insurance, whether on grant, on exercise, or on both. However, if the shares being offered under option are readily convertible assets, the *employer* must collect the tax due via PAYE. If the shares are not readily convertible assets, the *employee* is liable to pay the tax under the self-assessment regime.

As with the valuation of shares, the Inland Revenue takes the view that shares may become readily convertible before they are actually quoted, for instance when:

- the directors agree that the float will take place;
- knowledge of the planned float becomes public;
- the prospectus is issued.

Table 22.2 *Summary*

	Unquoted (including AiM and OFEX)	Quoted
Allowable ISA equity component holding	No	Yes
Allowable VCT holding	Yes if 'issued'	No
Loss relief available to set against income s574 ICTA 1988	Yes if 'subscribed for'	No
Holdover relief available on transfers at undervalue	Yes	Yes if 5% or more held
Business asset for taper relief	Yes	In some circumstances
EIS income tax relief/capital gains tax relief available		Yes No
Inheritance Tax Business Property (BPR) relief available	Yes (100%)	Yes (50%) if shareholder controls the company

STAMP DUTY ON THE FLOTATION

The general rule for Stamp Duty (and Stamp Duty Reserve Tax (SDRT)) is that the issue of new shares is not chargeable to duty.

An agreement to purchase existing shares will carry a charge to SDRT at 0.5 per cent of the consideration for the purchase. If stock transfer forms are required, then in practice Stamp Duty is paid on stamping the forms and this cancels the SDRT liability.

The structure of flotations can take a number of forms: perhaps the most common is an offer for sale. This can involve an offer of:

- pre-existing shares held by the shareholders; and/or
- newly issued bonus shares allotted to the existing shareholders; and/or
- new shares to be issued for cash to raise capital.

The offer may be implemented via an issuing house, and there are a number of stages to the offer with various transactions involving the issuing house, the company and new investors.

With careful structuring, the Stamp Duty (or SDRT) costs should be limited to the purchase of pre-existing shares by new investors. However, due to the resultant differing costs of acquisition of new and pre-existing shares, the vendor may agree to bear the Stamp Duty cost.

Index

Page references in *italics* indicate tables and figures.

BINNS & CO PR LTD

CORPORATE AND FINANCIAL PUBLIC RELATIONS

delivering your message

Flair and imagination, experience and professionalism ... at Binns & Co we draw on each of these elements to create an effective communications programme that adds value to your business.

London

16 St Helen's Place
Bishopsgate
London EC3A 6DF
United Kingdom

T: 020 7786 9600
F: 020 7786 9606
e: mail@binnspr.co.uk

Leeds

Russell House
St Paul's Street
Leeds LS1 2JG
United Kingdom

T: 0113 242 1171
F: 0113 234 9549
e: mail@binnspr.co.uk

We are a full-service, financial and corporate public relations and investor relations consultancy based in the City of London with a regional office in Leeds, and international affiliates in all of the world's key financial centres.

We offer commitment, continuity and a level of personal contact not often found in City PR firms. We pride ourselves on being client and service driven. We combine traditional people skills with a high degree of information technology.

www.binnspr.com